# From Upside Down To Rightside Up

*Cycle C Sermons for Lent and Easter
Based on the Gospel Lessons*

Wayne Brouwer

CSS Publishing Company, Inc.

Lima, Ohio

FROM UP-SIDE DOWN TO RIGHT-SIDE UP

FIRST EDITION
Copyright © 2021
by CSS Publishing Co., Inc.

**Library of Congress Cataloging-in-Publication Data:**
Library of Congress Cataloging-in-Publication Data

Names: Brouwer, Wayne, 1954- author. Title: From up-side down to right-side up : Cycle C sermons for Lent and Easter based on the gospel lessons / Wayne Brouwer. Description: First edition. | Lima, Ohio : CSS Publishing Company, Inc., [2021]
Identifiers: LCCN 2021002052 | ISBN 9780788030222 (paperback) | ISBN 9780788030239 (ebook) Subjects: LCSH: Bible. Gospels--Sermons. | Common lectionary (1992). Year C. | Lenten sermons. | Easter--Sermons. | Church year sermons. Classification: LCC BS2555.54 .B768 2021 | DDC 252/.62--dc23 LC record available at https://lccn.loc.gov/2021002052

For more information about CSS Publishing Company resources, visit our website at www. csspub.com, email us at csr@csspub.com, or call (800) 241-4056.

e-book:
ISBN-13: 978-0-7880-3023-9
ISBN-10: 0-7880-3023-X

ISBN-13: 978-0-7880-3022-2
ISBN-10: 0-7880-3022-1                                                    DIGITALLY PRINTED

For
Eva, Abby, & Noah
Alexa & Reed
Ellabelle


"One generation commends God's works to another..."

Psalm 145:4

# CONTENTS

# Foreword

Chris was called to ministry. He knew it. He felt it. He prayed about it.

But before he could be credentialed as a pastor, Chris had to channel his passionate confidence through several years of seminary training. Bible classes were great and theology courses were mostly interesting, although Chris never imagined that basic beliefs could be so nuanced and complicated. What he feared, however, was that first preaching class.

His group met once a week in the seminary chapel. Each student was assigned a date on which to present her or his first attempt at exhorting to the others — "practice preaching", they called it. Despite his past times of speaking about his faith, this challenge seemed to overwhelm Chris. When he got to the pulpit on his turn up front, he froze. He could not focus on his notes. He shook with fear so badly that if his hands were not gripping the edges of the podium, he would have collapsed.

The homiletics professor nodded at him and smiled encouragingly. After several moments of quivering silence, however, Chris' classmates began to shift uncomfortably. The professor said a few words, first gently and then more firmly, nudging Chris to get on with it.

But the sermon was stuck somewhere Chris could not retrieve it. Finally, in desperation, he stuttered out a question, "D-d-d-do y-y-you kn-kn-know what I am going to s-s-say?"

They did not have a clue, of course, and every head wagged from side to side. Chris ran for the door and escaped the building.

The professor was concerned. He summoned Chris to his office. They talked about nerves, techniques, and preparation. Then he told Chris, "You are up again next Tuesday."

The maelstrom of swirling fear tightened. Chris hardly slept, and he practiced in the empty chapel early each morning before anyone else arrived at the seminary.

Class time arrived too soon and Chris was back at the pulpit. But it was a repeat disaster. White knuckles, shivering panic, and another stuttered question: "D-d-d-do y-y-you kn-kn-know what I am going to s-s-say?"

By this time, all in the class could see that Chris had reached his public speaking capacity again, so all nodded. "Good," said Chris with relief. "Then I don't have to tell you!" He made his same door dash and was gone before anyone could move.

The professor was on the edge of irritation. He called Chris into his office again, and the words were stern and direct. Chris would present on Tuesday or he would fail the course.

Tuesday came… Same setting, same circumstances, same stymied student. Even the same stuttered query: "D-d-d-do y-y-you kn-kn-know what I am going to s-s-say?"

Those in the chapel no longer knew what to think, so some doubters shook "No" while others who saw a repeat non-performance coming nodded "Yes."

"Okay," Chris squeaked. "Those of you who know, tell those of you who don't!"

### Familiar Gospel

It never happened to me quite that way but I am a fearful and timid preacher. I have spent decades doing this thing I know God has called of me and from me. Yet every worship service is a new challenge, with shaking knees, evasive notes and memories of what I have prepared, and a sense that these gathered people should really be doing something more important than listening to me.

Still, I am convinced that preaching matters, and that the spoken word, transmitted through a believing heart and a passionate mind is one of the most persuasive experiences any of us can have. I keep praying and preparing. And when the opportunity to lead worship and bring the message is there, I do what I can to tell again the most incredible story in all its transforming dimensions.

I hope these attempts at capturing preaching on the page are beneficial for you.

All the best…

Wayne Brouwer

Ash Wednesday

**Matthew 6:1-6, 16-21**

# A Portion Of Thyself

At a graduation ceremony, the president of a Christian college stood at the podium and looked out over the huge crowd of people. He shook his head and said to himself (right into the microphone, of course!): "All these Christians in one place, and no one's taking an offering!"

We take offerings a lot, don't we? Every Sunday at worship services, the money plates are passed. In fact, we can hardly think of a meeting of Christians where there is not some suggestion about offerings, donations, or contributions. Money and religion seem to go hand in hand.

Indeed, someone told a story of an airplane that was experiencing problems. One of the engines had failed, and another was acting strange. The passengers were getting nervous. Some were beginning to panic. Finally, one fellow sitting near the front of the plane yelled out, "Is there a priest or a minister on board who can do something religious?!" There was; a clergyman got up, and passed his hat for an offering!

Money and religion often go hand in hand! But maybe they should. They certainly did for Jesus. The gospels record 37 of his parables, and in nearly half of them — sixteen, to be exact — Jesus talks about money and the way in which we use our possessions!

More than that: one-tenth of all the verses in the gospels deal directly with the subject of money. That's 288 verses! Again, when you look at the whole Bible, you find that less than 500 verses speak specifically about faith, and only 500 verses talk about prayer, yet more than 2,000 verses address the topics of money and possessions!

# From Upside Down to Rightside Up

Religion and money go hand in hand. Of course, that is essentially what Jesus is saying in these verses; "Your money and your religion go hand in hand! Your faith and your finances are part of the same package! What you do with your checkbook is as important as what you do with your Bible!" Religion and money go hand in hand.

In that light, there are three questions we must face.

### Are You Aware?

The first is this: "Are you aware?" Do you see others around you? Has your faith opened your eyes to the need and the concerns of your partners in the human race?

Probably no period in human history was as peaceful and as prosperous as the days of Antonius Pious (138-161 AD), who ruled Rome in the second century. Edward Gibbon, in his magnificent treatise *The Decline and Fall of the Roman Empire,* said that the times of Antonius Pious were the "happiest" on earth. He was probably right. There was more wealth and business success and domestic peace in those days than most civilizations have ever known.

Antonius Pious was a good ruler and his people knew it. In fact, one of his biggest supporters was the Athenian philosopher Aristedes. Aristedes couldn't seem to write enough verses in praise of Antonius. He lauded the government, and the beauty of Rome. He praised the magnificence of its buildings and the character of its citizens. Aristedes was a one-man ministry of propaganda, telling the world of the pomp and splendor of Antonius Pious and his great government.

But Aristedes wrote about other things as well. One day, he sent a letter to Antonius, telling the monarch to keep his eye on a certain group of people in his empire. "You need these people," said Aristedes. "You should find them and talk with them. You can learn much from them."

"The unique thing about them," said Aristedes, "is that they really have eyes to see others. They watch out for those around them. They take care of the widows, who are often pushed aside when their husbands die. They look after orphans, especially those who get sold as slaves. These people will even pay huge sums of money to buy the freedom of others."

It is not that these folks are so wealthy. In fact, said Aristedes, they are often the very poor of most Roman cities. Yet if they know of someone in need, they will even go without food for two or three days in order to save a few coins that might help someone else.

"You should get to know these people, Antonius!" said Aristedes. "In all your grand empire, they are the only ones who make it a habit to see the needs of the poor and do something about it."

Who was Aristedes writing about? Christians! He was writing about the followers of Jesus! Can you imagine it? A Greek philosopher telling one of the greatest Roman emperors to look for Christians because they were the ones from whom he could learn something!

So it is appropriate for Jesus' followers always to ask one another, "Are you aware?" Do you see? Have you reached beyond yourself and looked at the lives and the circumstances of your partners in the human enterprise?

In 1966, evangelist Martin Higgenbottem was one of the main speakers at the Berlin World Congress on Evangelism. He told the gathering that his life of devotion and service had to do with his mother. He remembered coming home from school one afternoon to find her sitting at the kitchen table with a strange man. The fellow was obviously someone who lived on the streets. His clothes were filthy, his hair was slicked with unwashed grease, his body smelled of a mixture of unkind odors.

But Martin's mother was chatting pleasantly with him while they devoured a plate of sandwiches together. She had gone shopping that morning and found him cold and hungry, so she brought him home with her.

When the man was ready to leave, he said passionately, "I wish there were more people in the world like you!"

Martin's mother casually threw the compliment aside. "Oh," she said, "there are! You just have to look for them!"

## From Upside Down to Rightside Up

The man broke down. He shook his head, and tears rolled across his cheeks. "But lady!" he said, "I didn't have to look for you! You looked for me!"

You looked for me! "Are you aware?" asks Jesus. Are you aware?

### Will You Share?

A second question follows: "Will you share?" Will you take what you have and give to those around you? Will you use your blessings to touch the lives of others?

There is a wonderful story told about Fiorello La Guardia, mayor of New York City during the Great Depression. Before he became mayor, he served for a time as a police court judge. One cold winter's day, a man was brought before him was charged with stealing a loaf of bread. La Guardia asked if he was guilty. The man nodded. He had taken the bread because his family was starving, and he had no money to buy food. What was he to do?

The law bound La Guardia. "I've got to punish you," he told the thief. "The law makes no exceptions! I fine you $10!" And he brought down his gavel.

But where would the man get the money for the fine? Now they would have to throw him in jail as well!

La Guardia wasn't finished, though. He already had his hand on his wallet. He pulled out a ten-dollar bill, handed it to the bailiff and said: "Here's the money for your fine."

Then he took back the ten dollar bill, put it into his hat, handed the hat to the bailiff and said, "I'm going to suspend the sentence, and I'm going to fine everyone here in the courtroom fifty cents for living in a town where a man has to steal bread in order to eat!"

When the man left the courtroom, he had the light of life in his eyes and forty-seven dollars and fifty cents in his pocket!

"Will you share?" Will you share what God has given you with others around who have needs today?

It was a requirement of the Jewish religion to give alms for the poor. That's what Jesus was talking about in the verses of Matthew 6. In fact, the Old Testament rules and regulations had a built-in system that guaranteed help for the poor. You were not even allowed to come to the temple for worship unless you had given alms to the poor.

Tithing was a standard practice. One tenth of everything you ever earned was to be given back to God as a confession of faith. But how can you give money to God? Do the deacons take the offerings and go into the back room of the church and toss it all up to heaven, and whatever God doesn't want falls back to the floor?

No, God's instructions were very clear. When you give your tithes to the poor, he said, you are giving them to me! Jesus echoed that idea in a later teaching. In Matthew 25 he talked about the end of time, and the day we will all appear before the throne of God for judgment. God will say to some of us: "You took care of me! When I was hungry, you fed me. When I was naked, you clothed me. When I was sick, you looked after me."

We'll shake our heads, according to Jesus, and have this puzzled look on our faces. We'll say to God: "When was that? I don't remember ever seeing you on earth! When did we help you out like that?"

The Father will look at us, Jesus said, and he will say: "When you gave to the poor among you, when you offered help to those who needed it, when you went beyond yourself in mercy, you did it to me!"

We don't always do well at that, do we? The Internal Revenue Service tells us that few of us even admit to giving for charitable causes. Americans give only about 1.65% of their incomes to charity! That included *all* charitable causes, like the arts, universities, hospitals, and cultural centers! That's 85% *less* than tithing!

It's not that we are isolated from the needs in our world. We hear the news, we see the pictures, we are challenged by the requests that come every day in the mail. When Jesus asks us, "Are you aware?" we can only say, "Yes! Painfully so! Enormously so!"

But when Jesus asks us, "Will you share?" that's a different story. We are programmed to take rather than give. We are taught by our society to receive, but not necessarily to share. We are challenged by our aged to grab for all the gusto we can get and not to deprive ourselves of anything for the sake of others.

John Bright, a British politician of the nineteenth century, was walking down a street one day when a fellow was seriously injured in an accident. The crowds gathered around, gasping in delighted horror at the blood and the gore. But Bright took off his hat, grabbed a ten-pound note from his wallet, and stuffed it into his hat. Then he pushed his way through the crowds and said, "I'm ten pounds sorry for this man! How sorry are you?!"

In moments, he had turned the sickening curiosity of the people into sympathetic compassion.

Are you aware?

Will you share?

Those are the questions of Jesus for us.

### Do You Care?

Then comes the most important question of all. "Do you care?"

Do you really care about others? Is compassion a way of life for you?

Helmut Thielicke tells of a time he was hospitalized in great pain. The nurses were wonderful and took great care of him. One nurse, in particular, impressed him. She worked the night shift. Every evening she was there: prompt, pleasant, and efficient. She seemed to care deeply about her patients. She always had a bright smile for them.

In fact, in the sleepless hours of the night, she often sat next to Thielicke and talked with him. For twenty years she had been on this shift! For twenty years she had worked while others slept! She had given of herself in the darkest hours of the night.

"Isn't it a pretty stressful thing for you?" Thielicke asked her. "Don't you ever get tired of it all? How do you keep it up, year after year?"

Thielicke said she beamed at him, and this is what she told me: "Well, you see, every night that I work sets another jewel in

14

my heavenly crown! I already have 7,175 in a row!"

Thielicke said he was stunned! Suddenly his gratitude toward her was gone. She didn't really care about him! She wasn't helping him through his tough times because she felt compassion for him! She was only doing this in order to earn some kind of reward! Every night she kept count of her good deeds! Every smile was sold at a price! Every shift was a deposit in the bank of heaven, and that's all!

Sure, she was aware! Yes, she was willing to share! But did she care? Did her heart go with the gift? Did her spirit reach with her fingers and touch the one she tended? When she told the reason for her service, it seemed not.

Jesus talks in these verses about the rewards we get from God for the gifts of charity we give during our lives. Yet there is something crass and dirty when the rewards become our goals.

Some years ago, a man in Florida brought a lawsuit against his church. He demanded that the church return to him the $800 that he had given to it the year before. His court documents included this testimony: *"On September 7 I delivered $800 of my savings to the ( ) church in response to the pastor's promise that blessings, benefits, and reward would come to the person who tithed his wealth. I did not and have not received these benefits."*

You foolish man! Jesus would say. You silly beggar! Do you give in order to get? Do you tithe to earn a profit? Do you offer your services on the floor of the trading markets? Says one writer: "He that serves God for money will serve the devil for better wages!" (Sir Roger L'Estrange).

He is right! That is exactly Jesus' point. "Are you aware?" he asks us. "Yes!" we tell him. We see the needs around us.

"Will you share?" he requests of us. "Well, that's tough for us," we answer, "but we'll try."

Then comes the hard part. "But do you care?" Do you reach yourself with the gift? Do you touch the heart of the needy, and feel his hurts and know her wounds and stretch your hand in love and compassion? Do you care?

So often we don't even hear his question. We are too busy

asking a question ourselves: *What's in it for me? What do I get out of it? Will anybody notice? Do I get the "Good Citizen of the Year" award? Will there be a write-up in the papers?*

One man I know served in the church all his life. In his senior years, however, he became bitter. Nobody had ever really thanked him! None of the younger people in the church realized how much he had given! So he pulled back and wrapped himself in a security blanket of self-pity.

One woman's face was wet with tears when she came to see me. All these years she had volunteered her time and talents! Other women went out, got jobs, and earned money. But she always felt it was her responsibility to visit the needy to make meals for the poor, and to call on the sick at the hospital every week. Now she was tired of it all. Nobody cared what she had done! Nobody has ever stood up and thanked her publicly! Why should she give any more of herself if people were so ungracious?!

"Why indeed?" asked Jesus. If that's what it's all about, why indeed?

In C. S. Lewis' sermon *The Weight of Glory*, he talked about the idea of rewards in the Christian faith. He said, God promises us a reward for what we do in his name. But that doesn't make us mercenaries, giving in order to get, selling our good deeds on the open market.

If a man would marry a woman with great wealth in order to get her money for himself, said Lewis, we would call him mercenary, and rightly so! We would thumb our noses at him, and be appalled at his audacity!

But if a man marries a rich woman only because he expects the reward of love, said Lewis, we would think him the greatest fellow on earth! He would be getting his reward, but it would actually be the fulfillment of what he is himself giving to the other! His reward is the extension of his gift!

So it is with us, said Lewis. We give of ourselves in Christian charity. We give of our time, our talents, our money. And, as Jesus said, God will reward us.

But what will that reward be? A million dollars? A life without sickness or cancer? A public declaration of our good deeds?

No.

The reward is simply to become one with *love* itself, to give as we have been given, to share in the delights of his sharing, to stretch our souls and to find ourselves.

"I think," said Annie Dillard, "that the dying prayer at last is not 'please,' but 'thank you,' as a guest thanks his host at the door."

She was right. Life on earth is not about a demand for recognition, but a quiet "thank-you" for all that we have been able to see, show, and share.

That does not necessarily make good copy in the morning newspaper. Nor does it necessarily mean that we will be "successful" in life, at least in the ways many count success.

King Oswin, an early ruler of a northern territory in Britain, once gave his prize stallion to the local bishop as a token of appreciation. As the bishop traveled, he met a beggar along the road. Since the man had nothing at all, the bishop got off his fine steed and put the reigns in the man's hand. "Take him!" ordered the bishop. "Sell him and live! He's all I have to give you."

When King Oswin found out what the bishop had done he said, "Why didn't you sent him to me? We have dozens of old horses that are more fitting for a beggar!"

The bishop quietly asked, "Is that stallion worth more than a child of God?"

King Oswin thought about the question for a moment, and suddenly threw off his royal robes, falling at the bishop's feet and crying to God for forgiveness. The bishop blessed him and sent him away in peace. But for a long time he stared after the king with sorrowful eyes. When one asked him why he was so troubled, bishop Adrian replied: "I know that the king will not live long, for I have never seen a king so humble as he is. He will be taken from us, as the country is not worthy to have such a king."

His words proved true. In 651 AD, the king was murdered by a neighboring rival who used Oswin's own kindness to gain an audience. And the world was poorer that day.

But you are still here, and I am still here. And today we have heard again the questions of Jesus.

"Are you aware?" Do you see the needs of others around you? Are your eyes open to the plight of the poor and the troubles of the destitute? Are you aware?

"Will you share?" Will you take whatever God has given you, and put it at the disposal of others? Will you see your goods and property as a loan on deposit from God to be shared in his name as others call for it? Will you share?

"Do you care?" That most of all says Ralph Waldo Emerson: "Rings and jewels are not gifts, but apologies for gifts. The only gift is a portion of thyself." Is that the gift you give? Do you care? Does your heart stretch out with the love of Jesus? Does compassion flow in your veins? Have you found his reward in the act of love?

As we enter this season of Lent, walking in the servant footsteps of Jesus, we need to ask these questions. Am I aware? Do I care? Will I share?

First Sunday in Lent

Luke 4:1-13

# Into The Wilderness

Jesus was tempted.

We know the story is there, but it isn't our favorite, is it? Somehow it tarnishes our ideas about Jesus. Was he as wimpy as we are, almost ready to step over the edge of whatever morality we might have left, at the first offer?

Ray Stedman, great twentieth-century preacher, remembered a morning at a restaurant. He was the featured speaker at a large church conference out east and was finishing his presentation notes as he ate breakfast. The eatery had unique décor, including good quality and artfully fashioned pewter salt and pepper shakers on the tables along with matching creamers. Pastor Stedman knew that these would nicely complement his wife's collection. Every table had a set, so the restaurant obviously had more in its backroom storage. Pewterware cost a bit, but in volume like this they had to be a cheap item for the restaurant to replace.

Pastor Stedman knew he could slip the shakers into his briefcase and nobody would be the wiser. Still, being the man and the pastor he was, Reverend Stedman resisted temptation. Instead, he used the story as an illustration in his sermon the next Sunday morning, back in his California church. Yield not to temptation! Everyone smiled and nodded.

Four days later, however, a package was on Pastor Stedman's desk. Someone in his congregation decided to contact the restaurant, find out about the pewter tableware, ordered a set, and gave it to him anonymously as a show of appreciation.

The following Sunday morning he beamed appreciatively as he told his congregation about the special gift. They laughed together, and then he said, "I saw a great TV in a store this past week…"

Ahhh… temptations! They come in all forms, don't they? That is just as they did for Jesus.

### Why Is This Happening?

We are used to reading bits and snippets of biblical books, like this story of Jesus' temptations, in isolation from one another. Yet Luke intended that we hear the gospel as a whole, and that we keep this incident in its context. If we look at what lies on either side, we realize that Luke has at least three important ideas for us to understand as we think about Jesus' temptation. First, right from the beginning of this gospel every finger points to Jesus as a *phenom*, as a *wunderkind*, as a prodigy, as the "next great thing." He was born miraculously! He was feted by the great prophetic voices of the day! He confounded the scholars when he was only twelve, and his public coming out was shouted loudly by none other than the greatest religious figure of the day, John the Baptist. Jesus was the *next new thing*, and all the lights were pointing in his direction. When Jesus was tempted, we are keyed up to expect him to pull out his sword or light saber and slash his way to victory. But he did not. In fact, Jesus' way of dealing with these great evil threats seems almost trite and benign. Quote a few scripture verses? Turn his back on the devil? Saunter away as if nothing happened? Hmmmmm…

Second, Luke and the other gospel writers gave us big hints that Jesus was walking in the footsteps of Old Testament Israel. Jesus was tempted "in the wilderness," spending "forty days" there, just as Israel did between leaving Egypt and entering the promised land. Not only that, but the temptations themselves paralleled Israel's most challenging wilderness experiences:

- "We're starving, Moses! Make a miracle and give us food!"

- "We won against Pharaoh's army! We can be the most powerful nation in the world!"

- "God loves us! God will do anything for us!"

After forty days in the wilderness, Jesus was starving, Jesus was feeling the power of his connection with God, and Jesus was weakened enough to consider throwing himself on the "magic" of God's snap-of-the-finger, make-it-all-right providence. Like Israel in the wilderness, Jesus had been bounced around, experienced highs and lows, and was possibly ready to listen to any whisper of temptation that came along.

The third thing Luke wanted us to know was that this story was a foreshadowing of an ominous future. Notice again the premonition of more bad things to come that Luke used to close the episode: "When the devil had finished all this tempting, he left him until an opportune time" (Luke 4:13). Round one went to Jesus, said Luke, but round two and who knows how many more were still to come. The temptations would morph. They would snipe in at a different angle. The fight was not yet finished.

All three of these things — desperation, access to power, and success — were the key ideas Luke wanted us to focus on as we tracked with Jesus through this challenge. They were also the things Jesus wanted us to think about in ourselves, as he walked our walk with us.

### Desperation

It happens too often, doesn't it? Years ago, I watched a young couple bury three newborn sons in three successive years on foreign soil, far from family, despite the best efforts of medical science. In my career as a pastor, I have heard so many times the desperate cries of women who cannot get over the horrible pain of what fathers did to them in the secrecy of childhood bedrooms. I have seen robust faith degenerate through years of setbacks and loss.

Elaine Pagels, in retelling the story of a particular sect of early Christians, said, "History is told by the winners." There is a lot of truth in that. Who remembers the losers? Who keeps tabs on the has-beens? Who records the disasters of those who fade away under pressure or disaster?

# From Upside Down to Rightside Up

Because of the fickleness of our experiences and the frailty of our existence, our travels are rarely even keel. We rise to heights of ecstasy. We drop to "sloughs of despond," as Bunyan put it in *The Pilgrim's Progress*. We ride the roller coaster with its cheers and fears, some of them deeply disturbing.

We had a moment of that desperation in our family years ago. There was a section in one of our city parks called "Storybook Gardens." It was a children's village filled with scenes from nursery rhymes and fairy tales. There were animals to touch, feed, and watch, as well as playgrounds for jumping, running, and climbing.

There was also a maze. It was made of four-foot fencing covered by opaque canvas, a human puzzle full of blind alleys and dead ends. Our girls ran right on into the maze when we first saw it. Kimberly dashed ahead, banging about this way and that, and finally blundering her way through by trial and error. But Kristyn and Kaitlyn got stuck and trapped. The walls closed in on them. There was no way out. Suddenly, a desperate crying and fearful wailing rose above the maze! And Daddy, who could see all things, had to rescue them from the melancholy of the maze!

## The Maze Of Melancholy

There are times in all our lives when we enter the "maze of melancholy." We feel weak, helpless, and lost. The walls start closing in around us. There is no future and no past — just the hopeless grim skies of now.

We see Jesus there, in this wilderness spot of temptation, and know that this will not be the last time. It reminds me of the songs of William Cowper, a member of John Newton's congregation in Olney, England, in the 1700s. Some of his poetry has found its way into the classic hymnals of the church. "God moves in a mysterious way, his wonders to perform," says one song. Another declares, in a wonderful confession of confidence:

*What God ordains is always right; he guides our joy and sadness.*
*He is our life and blessed light; in him alone is gladness.*
*We see his face, the way of grace; he holds us in his mighty arm*

*and keeps us safe from every harm.*
(in the public domain)

But William Cowper was a troubled soul. He began to slip in and out of depression. He spent a year and a half in what was then called an "insane asylum." His hymns began to take on a darker color. During those bleak times, he penned this cry of spiritual loneliness:

*Where is the blessedness I knew, when first I sought the Lord?*
*Where is the soul-refreshing view of Jesus and his word?*
(in the public domain)

Cowper died of a broken heart and a crushed spirit. Sometimes we want to die, too, stranded in our own "maze of melancholy."

Yet the only way out is through, as Jesus shows us. Scripture is our link to heaven's resources: light in the darkness, stability over shifting footfalls, strength when muscles give out, resilience against temptations.

Early last century, Tommy Dorsey, the "blues" songwriter and musician, had a moment when the world had collapsed around him, and he wandered in his private "maze of melancholy." He sat at his piano and wrote this little prayer: "Precious Lord, take my hand…." Read through those lyrics.

We know that place, don't we? We cry with him: Lord – take me to be with you.

Or, with Jesus, we affirm that we only find our way, "by every word that comes from the mouth of God."

### The Lure Of Success

But sometimes the temptations do not crowd us in or trap us in desperation. Instead, they promise us the world. "Just do this, and you will get what you know you deserve!" "Just sign here, and we will guarantee you a win!"

Maurice Boyd, a former colleague of mine, pastoring the church down the street, remembered an incident that sealed the impact of his father on his life forever. Boyd's father worked in a shipyard in Belfast, Northern Ireland. During the Great Depression, work dried up. Times were tough and for three years his father was out of a job.

Then one of his father's old bosses at the shipyard approached him. This important and connected man would find work for Mr. Boyd. He could guarantee it, no matter how much worse things got. All Mr. Boyd would have to do would be to buy a life insurance policy from the man. It would work to their mutual benefit: the boss's income would increase, and Mr. Boyd's work income would be guaranteed!

It was a great deal, except for one thing: it was illegal. Maurice Boyd remembers his father sitting at the kitchen table with the whole family surrounding him. There his father counted the cost. He reviewed their desperate financial situation. He ticked off the outstanding bills and the money he would be making, *ought* to be making, if only he said yes to his boss.

Boyd's father wrote it all down on a sheet of paper: the gains and the losses, what he could make and what he could lose. Then he wrote down a category that Maurice Boyd would never forget: integrity. Integrity - what did it matter if he gained the cash to pay the rent, but lost his ability to teach his children right from wrong? What did it matter if he gained the dignity of a job but lost it each morning when he looked at himself in the mirror and knew that the only one reason he could go off to work instead of someone else was because he cheated?

Boyd's father declined the job and the family groveled through several more years of poverty. Yet, of his father, Maurice Boyd said, "He discovered that no one can make you feel inferior without your consent, and that one way you can keep your soul is by refusing to sell it. He realized that whatever else he lost … he didn't have to lose himself."

Where did Boyd's father get an idea like that? He got it from Jesus. From Jesus, who pushed back against the devil in the wilderness, knowing that the shortcut did not end up at the same destination. Yes, Jesus deserved the acclaim of the crowds and the kingdoms. Yes, Jesus wished for reconciliation between heaven and earth that did not come at such a bloody price. Yes, Jesus desired to remount the throne of glory without passing through Gethsemane. But that would be an alternate reality. That would be a fairy tale in which "they lived happily every after" by bedtime.

And we know it too.

### The Greatest Seduction

But the last temptation was the hardest, wasn't it? No longer desperate, clear-headed and strong, Jesus seemed to be a double winner. That is precisely where evil brought its last seduction.

"You have faith! You have great faith!" Trust God! Live as if it matters!

Here is where the insidious call of the "health and wealth gospel" summons. God wants you to have it all! You don't have because you don't ask! Prove your faith by your works!

Yes, yes, yes. A young couple started worshiping with my first congregation. They were members of a church in a nearby town, but they said they were looking for more; more spirituality — more life — better preaching — sincere worship. So they came to join us.

I met with them, wanting to get to know them. I also basked in the accolades they gave. I ate it up.

Then came the hook. This couple had been married for more than two years but did not yet have children. They wanted to have babies, lots of them. They believed that they were destined to have a large family. In fact, they had kept themselves pure before marriage, knowing that God would bless their union. It was biblical.

Here they were with me. Could I pray for them to get pregnant? After all, I was a "spiritual" man. They could see it! I prayed. I prayed fervently.

And they believed. Each Sunday she came to worship wearing maternity dresses, proving her faith to God, to me, and to the church.

But the pregnancy did not happen. For whatever reason, they remained childless. In a short while, they disappeared from our community. Someone who knew them well said that they were now worshiping with another congregation where the new minister was a firebrand. It was another place where they could prove their faith in an even more dynamic way.

The lure of success says to be pious! It says to have faith! Throw yourself into a dangerous situation, said the devil, and God will send angels to protect you!

And still we have to live. There is something low-key and tame about how Jesus got through this wilderness wandering, just as it was for the Israelites. Keep walking. Keep trusting. And keep your faith.

The tests continue. The exam is long. But grace abounds.

### The Armor Of Humility

Thomas Long told about the process of examining seminary students for ordination in a Presbyterian church in North Carolina. The students needed to pass an intense examination out in the church somewhere. The ministers in the area got to grill a student on any point of theology for as long as they wished, and sometimes the questioning lasted a long time.

Thomas Long said that one of his clergy colleagues who had served the same congregation for more than thirty years sat in silence throughout those ordeals. He never said a word, never asked a question, never demanded a clarification, until the very end.

Then, just when the examinations seemed to have run its course, the questioners were getting tired, and the seminary graduate started to think the ordeal was over, this gentleman stood. "Look out there," he said. He pointed to a large window at the side of their meeting hall. "Tell me when you see someone walking out there."

The candidate sat there, neck craned, and looked for a while. "I see someone," he said.

"Do you know the person?" asked Long's friend.

"No, I don't."

Said the elderly gentleman, "Describe that person to me, theologically."

This sage of North Carolina claimed that one of two reasons was always given. When you sift through all the academic lingo and verbal padding, some seminary graduates said something like this: "There goes a sinner who's on his way to hell unless he repents and gives his life over to Christ."

The other answer went something like this: "There goes a person who is a child of God. God loves that person so very much, and the best thing that can happen to him is to find out how good it is to love God in return."

"They're both right," said the elderly man behind the strange question. "That's what the scriptures and the church have always said. Still, as I've watched these fellows come and go over the years, the ones who answered my question the second way made better pastors. Mark my words!"

Do you believe it? If you do, then you probably have already peeked into the world of Jesus' wisdom in the wilderness of temptations. For when the roll is called up yonder, the grades on the report cards that make it won't be *A* for excellent, *B* for good, or even *C* for nice try.

The only grade that will make it will be *G* for grace.

Second Sunday in Lent

**Luke 9:28-36 (37-43a)**

# Mountaintop Experience

Some years ago, the History Network created a strange new hit series. It began as "Ice Road Truckers," monitoring the dangerous winter haulage north of Yellowknife on the frozen Canadian tundra. Then, after several seasons of gaining familiarity with the top tonnage truckers, the network displaced them to northern Alaska and introduced new challenges and new road masters. Finally, in a thrilling new twist, three of these rig lords and ladies were transported to the Himalayan heights of upper India. There the cameras panned, with toe-tingling shock and awe, the dizzying cliffs and switchbacks that painted tiny trails against massive mountains. One wanted to look up at splendor but became entranced by plummeting rocks and trucks bouncing toward seeming certain annihilation.

Yet if a trucker or traveler did reach the summit, all of heaven was at the doorstep. It was the top of the world — king of the mountain! It was truly a mountaintop experience.

It certainly seemed that way for Peter, James, and John as they scaled the upper altitudes of earth's crust that day, beckoned by Jesus to rise beyond this world into the next. What started out as a morning nature walk turned into a scenic climb. And then, before the day was over, the little group of friends fell upward into heaven.

Jesus glowed. Moses and Elijah came back to life. The voice of God thundered. We are all familiar with this story, aren't we?

But let's pay a little closer attention to the details as Luke recounted them. First, if we look at what Luke wrote before this, we realize that Jesus' Transfiguration came immediately on the heels of Peter's great confession of Jesus' identity. Only when

Jesus' disciples had begun to understand that their Master was more than merely one among many itinerant rabbis, that he was truly the promised Messiah, would their ministry of leadership in the age of the church take shape. What happened on the mountain of Transfiguration was simply that the testimony of Peter, received by the other and affirmed by Jesus, was now modeled before the intimate three. What God placed in Peter's heart to say publicly was suddenly displayed in living technicolor as heaven and earth kissed within the frame of Jesus' body. This was clearly Luke's understanding of the meaning of Jesus phrase "I tell you the truth, some who are standing here will not taste death before they see the kingdom of God" in verse 27, as the prelude to this amazing event.

Second, it is important to note that Jesus did not give up his humanity while expressing his divinity, nor did he become unknown in his divinity so that his humanity was obliterated. The Transfiguration was one of the most impressive Christological moments in Jesus' earthly life, when the fullness of deity became obviously human and the fullness of humanity became unquestionably divine. It was a mystery, of course, but it was the reason why the Nicene Creed (birthed out of the Councils of Nicaea in 325 and Chalcedon in 451) placed the specific limits that it does to our understanding of the natures and person of Jesus.

Third, the appearances of Moses and Elijah were critically instructive. How were Peter, James, and John to know the identity of these two figures who suddenly materialized before them? Probably Jesus told them, or the voice from heaven made it obvious. In any case, they knew, and we know that these two were the faces of the Bible in their times. Moses represented "the law." He was the mediator of the Sinai covenant that was responsible for Israel's national identity and missional purpose on behalf of Yahweh. Elijah, on the other hand, was "the prophets." Elijah stood at the head of the prophetic line, whose teachings would make the Sinai Covenant a living constitution for the shape of Israel's life. By the time of Jesus, only the "law" (that is, the first five books of today's Hebrew Bible, those commonly identified as the books of Moses or the Torah) and the "prophets" (the prophetically interpreted histories of Israel found in Samuel and Kings, and the great scrolls of Isaiah, Jeremiah, Ezekiel, and the twelve) were received as authoritative scripture. The "writings" collection would not be finalized until decades later. Moses and Elijah were the fountainheads of the two acknowledged collections of divinely inspired scripture. Appearing with Jesus, as they did, Moses and Elijah confirmed that the entire word of God pointed to Jesus and was fulfilled in Jesus.

Fourth, Peter's desire to turn the site into a new religious shrine, and Jesus' refusal to allow that to happen, was a reminder of the gospel's expression of Jesus' journey. This was only a transitional point, not a conclusion to things. The necessary revelation was not that Jesus *had* fulfilled the law and the prophets, but that he *was* the fulfillment of the law and the prophets, something that is still underway.

Fifth, the voice from heaven was an external confirmation that this was more than just a dream or hallucinogenic vision. This encounter had substance and it had a purpose. Once the three had seen more fully who Jesus was, they carried with them an added responsibility to treat him with appropriate respect and to safeguard the mission that he was on. Increased knowledge brings heightened responsibility.

Sixth, immediately after the "mountaintop" exhilaration of the Transfiguration, life took a rather grim turn. They headed down the mountain with warm joy in their hearts, only to feel the crush of real life in the valley below. Down here the demons ruled. Down here the world was torn by evil. Down here there were pains and torments. Down here, the kingdom had not yet become prominent. Moreover, the disciples who were not on the mountain with Jesus were weak and helpless. They did not have any power in themselves to change things. Jesus, of course, had the power, but his range of influence was limited by his conjoined divine and human natures, so that he could not be everywhere at once. He was able immediately to cast out the demon and heal the boy, restoring one small beachhead of the kingdom here. Even so, the other disciples, and those who came to the radiance of the glory of God through them, still needed taught. The Transfiguration was a turning point, a transitional statement. It pointed to the need for Jesus to finish his work so that its effects might be transferred into the expanding army of grace that would be generalled by these officers in training.

### Light In The Darkness

Here and throughout the New Testament theme there was a strong message that our world is very dark, and that Jesus is the light of God penetrating earth's blackness and bleakness. It is the message that the Christian church was and is the lingering glow of divine radiance pushing the transformations of heaven a little further through recessed corners of shame and pain. How are we glowing today?

Think of the ancient legend first told by Christians living in the catacombs under the streets of Rome, that pictures the day when Jesus went back to glory after finishing all his work on earth. The angel Gabriel met Jesus in heaven and welcomed him home. "Lord," he said, "Who have you left behind to carry on your work?"

Jesus told him about the disciples: the little band of fishermen, farmers, and housewives.

"But Lord," said Gabriel, "what if they fail you?! What if they lose heart, or drop out?! What if things get too rough for them, and they let you down?"

Jesus repied, "Then all I have done will come to nothing!"

"But don't you have a backup plan?" Gabriel asked. "Isn't there something else to keep it going, to finish your work?"

"No," said Jesus, "there was no backup plan. The church was it. There was nothing else."

"Nothing else?" asked Gabriel. "But what if they fail?"

And the early Christians knew Jesus' answer. "They won't fail, Gabriel," he said. "They won't fail!"

Isn't that a marvelous thing?! Here are the Christians of Rome, dug into the earth like gophers, tunneling out of sight because of the terrors of Nero up above. They are nothing in that world! They are poor, despised, and insignificant! Yet they know the promise of Jesus: "You won't fail! You're my people, and you won't fail!"

It is like the story Tony Campolo once told of a friend of his who was walking through the midway at a county fair when he met a tiny girl. She was carrying a great big fluff of cotton candy on a stick, almost as larger as herself! He said to her, "How can a little girl like you eat all that cotton candy?!

"Well," she said to him, "I'm really much bigger on the inside than I am on the outside!"

So it is with us. On the outside, we seem to be nothing, like Jesus' helpless disciples below the mountain of the Transfiguration, but on the inside, we are as big as the kingdom and the power and the glory of your God.

Transfiguration — transformation — what would our neighborhood be without us? What would our area be like without the church of Jesus Christ? Where would our nation be without the conscience of the people of God? It is not enough to be anti-abortion; you must be pro-life, and remind your community what real life, God's life, is all about! It is not enough to be against immorality; you must be the conscience of society, turning its thoughts toward love and laughter and life! It is not enough to protect your own interests; you must speak out for the welfare of the poor and the disabled and the oppressed!

There is a marvelous little story tucked away in the pages of Edward Gibbon's seven-volume work, *The Decline and Fall of the Roman Empire*. It tells of a humble little monk named Telemachus living out in the farming regions of Asia.

Telemachus had no great ambitions in life. He loved his little garden and tilled it through the changing seasons. But one day in the year 391, he felt a sense of urgency, a call of God's direction in his life. Although he did not know why, he felt that God wanted him to go to Rome, the heart and soul of the empire. In fact, the feelings of such a call frightened him but he went anyway, praying along the way for God's direction.

When he finally got to the city, it was in an uproar! The armies of Rome had just come home from the battlefield in victory and the crowds were turning out for a great celebration. They flowed through the streets like a tidal wave and Telemachus was caught in their frenzy and carried into the coliseum.

He had never seen a gladiator contest before but his heart sickened. Down in the arena, men hacked at each other with swords and clubs. The crowds roared at the sight of blood and urged their favorites on to the death.

Telemachus could not stand it. He knew it was wrong; this wasn't the way God wanted people to live or to die. Little Telemachus worked his way through the crowds to the wall down by the arena. "In the name of Christ, forbear!" he shouted.

Nobody heard him, so he crawled up onto the wall and shouted again: "In the name of Christ, forbear!" This time the few who heard him only laughed. But Telemachus was not to be ignored. He jumped into the arena and ran through the sands toward the gladiators. "In the name of Christ, forbear!"

The crowds laughed at the silly little man and threw stones at him. Telemachus, however, was on a mission. He threw himself between two gladiators to stop their fighting. "In the name of Christ, forbear!" he cried.

They hacked him apart! They cut his body from shoulder to stomach and he fell onto the sand with the blood running out of his life.

The gladiators were stunned and they stopped to watch him die. Then the crowds fell back in silence, and, for a moment, no one in the coliseum moved. Telemachus' final words rang in their memories: "In the name of Christ, forbear!" At last they moved, slowly at first, but growing in numbers. The masses of Rome filed out of the coliseum that day, and the historian Theodoret reported that never again was a gladiator contest held there! This was all because of the witness and the testimony of a single Christian who had the glow-in-the-dark power of grace and God's goodness.

### Lingering Glow

During the time of the Reformation, John Foxe of England was impressed by the testimony of the early Christians. He gleaned the pages of early historical writings and wrote a book that has become a classic in the church, *Foxe's Book of Martyrs*.

One story he told was about an early church leader named Lawrence. Lawrence acted as a pastor for a church community. He also collected the offerings for the poor each week, and that led to his death.

A band of thieves found out that Lawrence received the offerings of the people from Sunday to Sunday, so one night, as he was out taking a stroll, they grabbed him and demanded the money. He told them that he did not have it, that he had already given it all to the poor. They did not believe him and told him they would give him a chance to find it. In three days, they would come to his house, and take from him the treasures of the church.

Three days later they did come, but Lawrence was not alone. The house was filled with the people of his congregation. When the thieves demanded the treasures of the church, Lawrence smiled. He opened wide his arms and gestured to those who sat around him. "Here's the treasure of the church!" he said. "Here's the treasure of God that shines in the world!"

Indeed! As Jesus said in another place, "You are the light of the world." You can glow in the dark of this world, shining the light of the Transfiguration to those who desperately need it.

# Whose Fault Is It?

The youth pastor at one of my former congregations had a cartoon taped to his office door. It pictured a little guy standing, trembling, in front of a massive desk behind which was sitting a big, big man. The little guy wore torn jeans and a T-shirt, and had a leather loop around his neck holding a cross in front of his chest. His hair was messy and his toes peeked out the front of his sandals. A stick-on name patch read, "Hi! I'm Mike! I'm the Youth Pastor."

On the dark and imposing desk was a bronze plate boldly proclaiming, "Senior Pastor." A caption underneath carried the senior pastor's booming message to his underling: "I DIDN'T SAY IT WAS YOUR FAULT; I SAID THAT I WAS GOING TO BLAME YOU FOR IT!"

### Blame Game

Something goes wrong and we need to point fingers, don't we? In tragedies, like those that happened while Jesus was teaching in Galilee, we need answers. The despotic ruler murders some opponents and people wanted Jesus to weigh in on the tragedy. But he would not take the bait. Instead, he turned the tables.

"You want to talk blame?" he countered. "What about when blame cannot be assigned, like when eighteen workmen died on the construction site; the tower collapsed right on them! Who are you going to blame? God?"

We are right in the crowd around Jesus, aren't we?

Cancer threatens. Why me?

Cars crash on the highways and relatives make little memorial gardens of crosses nearby. Why did it happen to them?

Some come back from war and others don't. And some who

come back are not the people they used to be. Who is at fault?

For some, the virus was a brief bout with a cold. For others it took half of families and left the original infectors unscathed. What kind of world is this?

In pandemics and poverty, in pain and politics, we want to point fingers. We need to assess blame.

### Birthed By Hurt

Probably no one has expressed these sentiments better than the novelist Peter De Vries. De Vries grew up in a Christian home but spent most of his life trying to sort out who God was to him. His most powerful novel, *The Blood of the Lamb*, was also his most tragic. It followed the career of Don Wanderhope.

Don's family believed in God. They trusted that God held all things in his hand, and they knew God would always be there for them. Don, however, did not find this to be the case. One tragedy after another dogged him, and he wished God would not pay so much attention to him.

At the climax of the story, Don's wife bore them a daughter, the one spot of grace in her father's otherwise troubled existence. After Don's wife took her own life, Don and little Carol forged a new life of grace together. But then, at the tender age of ten, Carol was diagnosed with leukemia. Treatments failed and Don desperately gave God another chance. Don went back to church and prayed for Carol, wasting away in the hospital. Don begged God to heal her, and to touch her life with relief and restoration.

But Carol died anyway. Don left the hospital carrying the birthday cake they were going to share at her bedside. Don walked past a church. Hanging over the doorway was a life-sized statue of Christ on the cross. Taking the cake in his hand, Don threw it at Jesus. Icing dripped from the face like blood.

That was Don's final prayer. That was what he thought of the God who betrayed him. That was his final pointing finger of blame.

### Job As Everyman

Have you been there? Many of us have. I've heard one refrain again and again during my years as a pastor: "Why did God let this happen? How could God do this to us? Why doesn't God hear my prayers?"

It is the cry of Job in the seeming meaninglessness of life made painful by compounded hurts. Do you remember the story of Job? He was one of the wealthiest men in the ancient world, with houses, servants, and treasures. He had more of everything than any person could covet.

Job was also a devout man, careful to renew his relationship with God each day. It seems, in fact, that God was rather proud of Job. When Satan came calling one time, God bragged to him about Job. "Have you seen my servant Job?" he asked. "Now *there* is a man whose heart you will never own!"

## Wagering

Satan was not so sure. He had cracked a lot of tough nuts in his time, and he took on Job as a special challenge. "Sure, Job loves you," Satan said to God. "But that's because you've bought his soul. You give him everything he wants. Why shouldn't he serve you? Even *I* would do that!"

That is when the wagering began, according to the Old Testament book. God gave Satan permission to take everything away from Job, stipulating only that Satan could not harm Job's own body.

So Job lost everything — his children, his flocks, his buildings, and his servants. He became as poor as a church mouse. Yet still Job loved God and served him openly.

The wagering in heaven heated up, and Satan got one more shot at Job in round two. He was allowed to touch Job's body without killing him. Job began to writhe in pain. And Satan touched Job's mind so that he could no longer clearly hear God's whisper of love. Job was all alone. His wife called him stupid, his friends called him a liar and a sinner, and the world did not even call him anymore. Outside, Job's horizons had collapsed. Inside he had become an echo chamber of despair. Where was God?

That is the hardest challenge in life, isn't it? I remember sitting with a mother in a hospital corridor, praying for the life of her daughter. The young woman was just beyond her teen years, and only a dozen months into marriage to a wonderful man. When the doctor assisted her delivery of her first child, he nicked something with his knife. Now the infant was turning every shade of yellow and gray and had been flown half-way across the country to get the best medical attention possible.

The mother was unconsolable. When we prayed, she felt no peace and could not find God. For three hours we watched her daughter's life slip away.

The mother stopped going to church. The young husband grew angry and did not know how to care for his young child. Where was God?

I hear his voice echoing that of Elie Wiesel, who endured the horror of the Nazi death camps. Wiesel watched women and children herded into gas chambers. He cried with men beaten down by cruel soldiers. He saw a young boy hanging on a gallows. "Where is God?" he cried.

The question of Job is asked in every generation: "Where are you God?" And often, as with Job, the only answer is silence. The promises of scripture become dead fantasies. The Holy Spirit leaves and the heart grows chilly. The newspapers report events that make no sense. Where is God? Where is God when a child dies? Where is God when a mother is snatched from her family? Where is God when nuclear reactors melt down, airplanes crash, and mines collapse? Where is God?

And Satan looked down from heaven with glee. He knew that he had Job then. He knew that he would never get out of that one. He knew the cards in his hand were the winning draw. Can faith remain when God is silent? Can trust carry on when there seems to be no one at the other end of the line?

"No!" shouted Satan. But *he* did not have the last world.

"Yes!" whispered Job. "Even though I cannot see him, even though I do not understand what is happening, even though every human wisdom tells me God's not there, I *know* that my redeemer lives, and with these eyes I shall see him!"

That is the deepest level of faith possible. This is what Jesus calls out to those who wonder and point fingers of blame in his community. There are no good answers. Job loves God not for what he gets out of it, but because it is the only way life itself makes sense. We trust in God not because we always feel the wonder of God's presence, but because, even in the most absurd turns of life, and the seeming absence of God, there is still truly nowhere else to turn.

### Back To Basics

This is why Jesus told his disciples to stop blaming and start thinking. We live in a compromised world where bad things happen, often to seemingly good people, and where logical equations of moral behaviors and expected reward outcomes leave us scratching our heads. We cannot figure out this thing. We cannot win the blame came. Ultimately, we do not find meaning and find fault in the same breath.

So Jesus said, "Ask yourselves how you are going to live in such a world." Stop pointing fingers and start grasping for meaning and hope. When the moment of crisis comes, whether along the journey or at the point of death, what will sustain us? What will bring stability out of chaos? Where can we find footing in the rushing and destabilizing currents of life?

Years ago, Dr. Arthur Gossip preached a sermon he called "When Life Tumbles In, What Then?" He brought that message on the first Sunday he returned to the pulpit of his congregation after his beloved wife had suddenly died. This was how he ended the sermon: "Our hearts are very frail and there are places where the road is very steep and very lonely. ...standing in the roaring Jordan, cold with its dreadful chill and very conscious of its terror, of its rushing, I... call back to you who one day will have your turn to cross it, 'Be of good cheer, my brothers, for I feel the bottom and it is sound.'"

Somehow, by the grace of God, when we stop pointing fingers of blame and start grasping heavenly hands, the perseverance of patience carries us through, and we know the end of the matter as did Job and Dr. Gossip. God will not leave us alone forever. God will answer our questions in time or eternity. God will resolve the problems of life's inequities and give us a future that Satan could never manufacture. The focus of faith carries us through, until we are no longer distracted by the unanswerable because our eyes have found a better place to look.

Sometimes, those who are new to faith know this best. L. Nelson Bell, the father-in-law of Billy Graham, was a medical missionary in China for much of his career. One of the earliest converts to Christianity under his ministry was a wizened old man that later church members simply called "Elder Cao." When Dr. Bell asked Elder Cao to tell some visitors why he had become a Christian, the elderly gentleman put it simply.

"A man fell into a deep and slimy pit," said Elder Cao, "and he was unable to get out. Along came the Buddha. He stopped and took pity on the man. 'If you will come up here to me,' said the Buddha, 'I will teach you the way of enlightenment and you will never fall into the pit again.' But the man could not get out of the pit, so the Buddha went on to bring enlightenment to others.

"Along came Confucius, and he too was moved with compassion by the plight of the man in the pit. 'If you will listen to my teachings,' said Confucius, 'you will understand how society is formed, and what can be done to prevent anyone from falling into the pit.' Then he, too, went on, for the man did not rise out of the pit.

"Finally," said Elder Cao, "Jesus came along. As with the others, he was filled with concern for the man in the pit. So he jumped down into the pit, and helped the man get out.

"This," said Elder Cao, "is why I am a Christian."

Fourth Sunday in Lent

Luke 15:1-3, 11b-32

# In The Mirror

The first birth is extraordinarily exciting, isn't it? My wife and I were married less than a year when our firstborn came along. We knew right away that she was the most beautiful, most intelligent, most promising human being that had ever come into this world!

Parenting the firstborn is an experiment in everything new. First smile, first coo, first steps, first words... One first we did not anticipate, however, was the first time our little Kristyn recognized herself in the mirror. We had often held her up in front of the mirror when we tried new outfits on her. "Isn't she cute?"

For many months, Kristyn did not "see" herself when we did this. We were enamored by her wondrous beauty but she did not lock eyes with her own image reflected back. She was not self-aware.

Then one day it happened. We held her in front of the mirror again and suddenly she knew she was there. She held her own gaze. She smiled herself into smiling and laughed herself into laughing. She jumped up and down on the counter with her little legs as we held her there. She saw herself for the first time.

### Reflected Identity

This is what happens to each of us when we read Jesus' stories in Luke 15. They are interesting. They are cute. They are captivating. But suddenly, as we scan these words again, we are caught staring at ourselves. Jesus held the mirror up to us, and we see ourselves.

At first we do not even realize it. After all, Jesus talked about sheep and the one that was lost. We are not sheep farmers. This

41

was a tale of folks who lived long ago and far away, wasn't it?

And then Jesus told the tale of a woman who lost a coin. It dropped and rolled out of sight. She crouched and looked, she swept and moved furniture. She pointed her light into dark corners. Finally, the coin winked, and she reached back into the dusty spaces to reclaim it. She threw a party, and welcomed all the neighbors, sporting her repaired jewelry as she hosted the event.

Then came the big story of a wealthy man with two sons. The older boy was a typical first child — rules and regulations, duty, hard work, rigor and righteousness. The younger son was a spoiled brat that always got what he wanted. He never had to work. He made those eyes and his parents melted all over him, even after party nights out with his friends, drinking, carousing, and destroying property.

The brothers clashed, obviously, and the hometown became too small for the worldly younger brat. He left home, coins jingling in his pocket. New friends "loved" him, as long as he was paying for everything. But one day the money ran out, and so did they.

Having never learned to earn his way, the wastrel became waste. Only an outcast immigrant farmer would pay him a few cents to do the dirty work every Jew thought reprehensible. He slopped the hogs and crawled up next to them at night.

In the wee hours of one restless morning, gnawing hunger in his belly and snorting hogs grunting their noisy dreams, he knew he had to head home. Not, mind you, as the proud son of his privileged family. He had lost that perch many types of bacon ago. No, he would grovel back, wimpering and crawling. His wealthy father sustained the local economy; surely there was a place for another hobo on the temp line.

Eyes were rolling and heads nodding as Jesus spun the story. Every family had a kid like that, every village knew its lost boys.

### An Unusual Turn

But then came the Jesus twist. You know he does that. He tells a story, and we get hooked. He weaved a tapestry of things we know, and we are right there with him. He went down a side road we did not even know was there! Suddenly we see things from a completely different perspective.

So here comes the Jesus twist. The father was not angry but welcomed his lost boy home. Dad even threw a homecoming party. Meanwhile, righteous older brother was incensed. He did not want to see his worthless brother again, let alone lose his special place as the one and only in his father's home.

When we go back and take a second look at these three stories, we realize that Jesus had been doing the "twist" all along. Think about these things:

- While we like to jump directly to Jesus' most famous story, the one we often call the "Parable of the Prodigal Son," we need to see that Jesus was deliberately stacking these three stories one on top of the other. They are related: a lost sheep, a lost coin, a lost person. We don't fully understand what Jesus wanted us to learn from the Parable of the Prodigal Son until we look at the other two parables that it is built upon.
- Second, we need to read the whole of Luke 15 to see the targets of Jesus' stories. Jesus was with the rejects of Jewish society, we are told, the "tax collectors and sinners." These were the lost people of that time, the outsiders who were not welcome at family gatherings or in places of worship. We might think that Jesus was telling these lost people that they could be found. That is what we would like to think. But notice that Luke told us something quite different was taking place: the religious leaders, Pharisees, and teachers of the law, happened by. They saw these social rejects, and they saw Jesus in the middle of them. They shook their heads and muttered about what a disgusting man Jesus was because of his association with those horrible nasties. At that moment, Luke said, Jesus turned to them, above the heads of the tax collectors

and sinners, and spoke the three stories to them. In other words, Jesus' parables in this chapter were not directed to "lost" people, but to "found" people; not to the outsiders but to the insiders; not to the rejects but to the self-righteous.

- Third, because few of us are middle-eastern sheep farmers, we may not catch the irony in Jesus' first story. Most flocks of sheep in that day would have been about five to twelve animals. A shepherd was typically a young boy, sometimes a young girl, or maybe an old man. There would be a personal bond between this little flock and the shepherd who served as their daily guide and protector. But Jesus told of a man who had one hundred sheep. In other words, he was referring to a very, very wealthy man, probably in his late middle years, who owned vast tracts of land and employed many servants. This man would not likely be the shepherd with the flocks. He would have hired young boys, young girls, or old men to do that. Nor would he likely know exactly how many sheep he owned on any particular day: some were being born, some were dying, some were being bought or sold, some were being eaten. But in Jesus' story, the very wealthy man not only knew how many sheep he had, but he was actively involved in the daily care of those sheep, and noticed when one little lamb was missing. More than that, when he realized a lamb had not returned to the sheep pen at the end of the day, he did not scold the hired shepherd of that particular flock within his herd, nor did he send that hapless youngster out to find the sheep he lost. Instead, the rich owner went on the quest himself, depriving himself of the rest and luxuries that he had a right to. Jesus was beginning to set the stage. He was not just talking about farmers in the area; he was making a clear analogy to God.

God is the great shepherd, like David said in Psalm 23. But even though God does not have to involve God's own self in our little and insignificant lives, God chooses to be personally invested in everything we are and everything we do. Remember — Jesus was speaking to religious leaders, who were expected to be shepherds of God's flock, and Jesus was speaking to those religious leaders as he sat among lost sheep! Hmmmmmm…. Perhaps God, the great wealthy owner of all the sheep was more concerned about the lost and the last and the least than are the local shepherds!

- Fourth, we are a bit perplexed about why a lost and found coin should be such a big deal, aren't we? Perhaps coins meant more back then than they do now. Jesus told us that it was a silver coin. Still, why should its loss be so serious and its recovery so significant that the woman threw a party when it was found? She likely spent more on food for her friends and neighbors than the coin was worth in the first place! But this only shows how far separated we are from Jesus' world. The coin was probably bored with a small hole near one edge. It had been slipped with nine other coins onto a leather thong as a necklace. Most certainly this had been given to the woman by her father as a wedding present. It was a testimony from her father of the great esteem he had for her. She wore the necklace every day. Everyone in the community knew it because they never saw her without it. So when one coin wore through to the edge and dropped off the leather thong, it was a serious matter. The necklace was incomplete, broken, less than what it was supposed to be.
- And if the woman ventured out into the market, or even spent time outside, greeting her neighbors, everyone would notice the lost coin immediately.

45

That is why she was so intent on finding the coin, restoring the necklace, and celebrating the recovery with her whole village. She was incomplete without it! Then Jesus made the nudge again: so it is with God when just one "worthless" sinner is found and brought back home. Everybody in heaven sings and laughs and has a party!

- And that brings us to the big store, the main event. The parable of the prodigal son. There is, again, more here than first meets the eye. Allow me to list a number of things we do not always catch, from our distant time and culture:

- First, the young son who asks for his inheritance is actually making a public declaration that he wishes his father would die. There was no "inheritance" before the parent had passed on! To ask such a thing was to spit in the face of the father and declare him worthless in the mind of the son!

- So what happened next? I want to know! You want to know! We all want to know! But Jesus did not tell us. He dropped the father's words on us like a blanket of love and then went quietly. He looked us in the eye until we grew uncomfortable. We do not know what to say, and Jesus will not say it for us.

**Seeing Ourselves For The First Time**

And that is where this parable, this unfinished story, becomes for us a mirror. Because we see ourselves for the first time, like our little daughter Kristyn did that day we held her in front of the reflective surface and she caught her own eye, when we look into this tale. We catch sight of ourselves first, in the selfish, stupid, sickened, and surprised eyes of the younger brother, the one who does not merit love and yet receives it from the father in abundance. We are the ones who come home to a father and a family we do deserve.

But wait! There's more! Remember the way Luke 15 began? Jesus was with one group of people when another group of people sauntered high-mindedly on by! Who was Jesus with? He was with the lost, the last, and the least. He was with the tax collectors, sinners, and prostitutes. Remember the words in the story? He was with people like the younger brother, the prodigal son.

And then, remember to whom Jesus told the three stories: the lost sheep, the lost coin, and the lost son? Not to the lost boys around him! No! He told the stories to the proud Pharisees and teachers of the law who strode on past, shooting daggers from their eyes at those worthless ones. He told the stories to the righteous religious people who knew they were better than everyone else. He told the stories to the older son, the older brother, and those like him, who disdained the ungodly and happy-go-lucky sinners of this world.

We think we see ourselves in the eyes of the younger brother, the prodigal son — and we do. But Jesus gently pointed our gaze in another direction, until we realize that we are not so much the younger son, the scandalous wastrel, as we are the old brother, the indignant, godly, righteous, holy, sanctified church people who have always done the right thing! We suddenly lock eyes with the older son and see our deeply dark and bitter and self-righteous souls. And we are shocked! We are indignant! And we complain to our Father that "grace is free, but it is not cheap," — that God should not lavish unrequited love on these terrible nasty folks who do not deserve it, like we do.

But Jesus held the mirror there long enough for us to recognize ourselves. Until all sanctimonious self-righteousness melted away in a muddy mess. And we were shocked at what we have become, who we thought we were, and what we really are.

And then... and then... and then came the strangest turn of all. Because the last gaze Jesus gave us, was to look into the powerful, tender, compassionate, gracious, loving eyes of our father — *our Father in heaven*. We are reflected there too, aren't we? We see ourselves in the mirrors of his eyes.

And we are loved.

# Terms Of Endearment

In his short story, "The Capital of the World," Ernest Hemingway reported an event they talk about in Madrid. A young man named Francisco, lovingly called Paco by his parents, grew to be a teen at odds with his father. No matter how a day began, it was sure to end with angry words and heated arguments. Paco and his father became enemies living under the same roof.

Finally the young man ran away, drifting eventually to the large metropolis of Madrid, where anyone could get lost and create a new identity. But relief from antagonism does not necessarily bring peace. Although free to find his own way, Paco was suddenly adrift in a world where many others tried to set his agenda, and missed the stability and resources of home. Meanwhile, back at home, his father and mother found themselves also in miserable silence. Paco's absence was more destructive than his petulant presence. They missed him terribly.

With passions only parents can know, Paco's father climbed the well-trodden roads to Madrid, asking all along the way if they had encountered his son. In the great city itself, the stranger wandered markets and main streets, seeking news of Paco. But not even in dimly lit dens and narrow alleys did anyone know about the missing teen.

Paco's father went to the office of "El Liberal," the largest newspaper in Madrid. He placed a personal ad that made this poignant promise: "Paco, meet me at Hotel Montana at noon Tuesday. All is forgiven. Papa."

The father could hardly sleep Monday night. Restless and hoping against hope, he arrived at the newspaper office already at mid-morning. By then, strange things were already beginning to happen in the street outside. Traffic was much heavier than anyone could remember, with an unusual percentage of young men milling about. By 11:00 that morning, the area was nearly clogged with pedestrians. Half an hour later, as the father scanned the roiling mass in hopes of spying his son, the Guardia had to be called out to control the mob. One observer from a second-story window reported that over eight hundred homeless Paco's had shown up, all hoping to find a loving father who would take them home.

### All Is Forgiven

This is the story of our gospel reading today. We are Mary, and Mary is us. Something had happened in her life that caused her to lose faith and hope until Jesus came along. Only through him was her soul restored, her psyche mended, and her trust nurtured back to life. There are many stories and legends that surround this passage, including thoughts that Mary had been a prostitute (drawing on parallels with other accounts and similar tales). We don't know. But what we are told with unbroken earnestness by John is that Mary's action in anointing Jesus startled all around her, including Jesus' own disciples. The act was too bold, too lavish, too emotional, and too over-the-top. Even Judas, who would not go down in history as the most careful of all men, was ready to shove Mary away as outlandish.

But Jesus would have none of it. He alone understood how close he was to his own death and welcomed the anticipated nod toward funereal honor. More than that, however, he honored Mary because of her passionate affirmation that Jesus meant everything to her. After the brokenness of life had washed her up, spit her out, and thrown her into the milling masses of Madrid, Jerusalem, Moscow, or Rio de Janeiro, Jesus was the word of the loving Father broadcast in mass media promising, "All is forgiven. Come home!"

This is why Jesus said we would remember her. Wherever the gospel is proclaimed, she is us, and we are her. When the transforming love of Jesus gives us the courage to express our appreciation, the world changes.

49

# From Upside Down to Rightside Up

## Transformational Love

Take, for instance, the story of Ernest Gordon's survival. Ernest Gordon's book *To End All Wars* (Zondervan, 2002) is the true tale of what took place in the Japanese prison-of-war camp made famous by the movie *The Bridge over the River Kwai*. The camp stood at the end of the Bataan death march that brought Allied soldiers deep into the jungles of Asia. Few would survive, and everyone knew it. In order to make the best of a terrible situation, they teamed up in pairs, each watching out for a buddy.

One prisoner was a strapping six-foot-three fellow built like a tower of iron. If any could come out of this alive, all felt he would. That was before his buddy got malaria. The smaller fellow was much weaker and very likely to die. Their captors did not want to deal with sickness, so anyone who was unable to work was confined in a "hot house" until he succumbed to heat exhaustion, dehydration, and the collapse of his bodily systems.

The sick man was locked into a hothouse and left to die. Surprisingly, he did not die, because every mealtime his strong buddy went out to him, under curses and threats from the guards, and shared his meager rations. Every night his strong buddy sneaked from the prison barracks, braved the watchful eyes above that held guns of death, and brought his own slim blanket to cover the fevered convulsions of the sick man.

At the end of two weeks, the sick man astounded the guards by recovering well enough to be able to return to work. He even survived the entire camp experience and lived to tell about it. His buddy, however — the strong man all thought invincible—died very shortly of malaria, exposure, and dysentery. He had given his life to save his friend.

The story did not end there. When Allied troops liberated that camp at the close of the war in the Pacific, virtually every prisoner was a Christian. There was a symphony orchestra in camp, with instruments made of the crudest materials. There were worship services every Sunday and the death toll was far lower than any expected. All this was because of the silent testimony made by a strong man toward his buddy facing death.

Only those who have been loved much can express it to others. Like Mary.

## Lost And Lonely

Dr. E. Stanley Jones related an incident from his missionary days that illustrated Jesus' point. A young girl got tired of things at home. She longed for the freedom of the streets and the excitement of the nightlife. She ran away to a large city. It wasn't long before she fell under the spell of a pimp and was degraded into a prostitute.

The girl's mother was beside herself with anxiety. It was true that things hadn't been going right between them, but a mother's love is restless and protective, and she had to find her daughter again. She remembered the child who sat on her lap, the daughter who whispered in her ear, and she now needed somehow to renew their bond of trust.

Yet how should she begin the search? All she had heard were rumors about daughter, third-hand reports that she was now wasting her body in the red-light district. The mother went to the city and simply began to walk, hoping to stumble across someone who might know her daughter. Up one street and down the next she trudged, talking to anyone who would listen, hoping for a clue to follow.

But to no avail. Her daughter did not want to be found: shame, rebellion, spite... Who can say what reasons mingle in our deceptive minds?

Eventually the quest tired even the mother. But before she returned home, she did one more thing. She carried a photograph that had been taken several years before, a picture of the two of them, mother and daughter, at a happier moment in both their lives. She got the photograph enlarged and made dozens of copies. Then she scattered those pictures around the area, hoping that one would catch her daughter's eye. On each photo she penned these five words: "Come home! I love you!"

And one day the girl did see. She began to remember what love was all about. A holy restless gripped her soul, battering her resentment until she had to call her mother. The next day, she was home.

Never once did the daughter stop assenting to the fact that she had a mother. But it was not until her mother's love called out the trust of her heart that she believed in all that "home," "mother," and "love" could mean to her personally.

There is much that we as disciples of Jesus can do in this world. We need to fight against consumerism. We need to give generously to churches and organizations which alleviate poverty and bring medical supplies to remote places. We need to help counter the craziness of society with acts of justice, mercy, and grace. We need to express compassion. We need to evangelize, to witness about the kingdom of God, and the righteousness of social justice. We need to fight against racism, elitism, cronyism, segregation, and Apartheid in whatever forms they raise their ugly heads.

But all of these things must begin at one place. We need to remember how much we are loved by Jesus. And we need to express our love back to Jesus in worship, devotion, and deep gratitude.

### Orphans No More

One couple I read about was filled with great passion, particularly for those orphaned in the many war zones of our world. We do not think much about the children, do we? We hear of battles, soldiers, guns, and attacks. But what about the children who could not sleep because of the booming of the bombs, who were left without parents in the storms of war, who had no food or water to sustain them when all supplies were cut off? What about the children who got sick from the poisonous fumes, whose limbs were blown away by the mines, and whose families had been scattered and deported? What about the children?

This couple thought about the children. They ached for the children. They worked tirelessly for the children. They wrote letters. They contacted government officials. They sponsored orphanages. They arranged for adoptions. They got interviewed constantly, in order to keep the tragedies alive. They traveled incessantly, all for the children.

One night, while they were holding another planning session in the living room of their home, the talk got noisy, and their five-year-old daughter appeared suddenly on the stairs, awakened by the loud bantering. Mother saw her and took her back to her room and bed. But the little one was crying.

"Hey, you're okay," Mom said. "I'm here. What's wrong?"

"Sometimes," the girl sobbed, "I wish I was an orphan. Then you would care about me like you care about the other children."

What a crushing heartbreak for that mother. To realize in all of her doing good, she had let the central relationship of her life lapse.

This is why Jesus pointed us to Mary. Judas said, "What a waste! We could have done so much with that money! We should get busy looking after the poor!"

Jesus did not dispute that. We need to help the poor.

But helping the poor, bringing justice to society, and evangelizing the world began with the one thing Mary got right. We need to love Jesus.

# Scandal

While Don Richardson was a student at Prairie Bible Institute in the 1950s, his heart burned in anticipation of bringing the good news about Jesus to an unreached tribe. He and Carol found their prayers answered in 1962 as they sailed out of Vancouver harbor toward Netherlands New Guinea. Before long, they were deposited by a missionary plane among the Sawi people, a group of tribes living in the trees of the interior rain forest.

The jungle floor was too damp for permanent dwellings, so the Sawi helped Don and Carol, and their infant son Stephen, build a tree house in their neighborhood. Carol learned the ways of the Sawi women while Don spent time with the men, attempting to understand their language and reduce it to writing. Afternoons would find the Sawi males in one of their treetop workrooms, buzzing in conversation while they mended nets and hunting equipment, and swapped stories of fish and boars.

It was in this setting that Don took his first furtive steps toward speaking the Sawi language and reciting stories from the gospels. Most of the time the others ignored him, caught up in their own manly concerns. The months progressed, and with little Stephen becoming a Sawi child, Carol adapted meals to local produce, and Don attempted to get the message of the Bible into a form the Sawi could understand.

### An Upsidedown Gospel?

But one day everything changed. Don was moving along in the gospel story to the last weeks of Jesus' life. As he related the tales about Jesus heading toward Jerusalem and the conspiracies that were swirling about him, the Sawi men began to listen. At first, it was only that their conversations with one another died down, while their hands continued in busywork with their hunting and fishing tools. But then even this work ceased, and every eye was fixed on Don. He happened to be talking about Judas' secret meetings with the religious leaders and the betrayal that ensued.

Suddenly there was a murmur of approval, and the delighted smiles of those who seemed to know this story. What is going on, Don asked his translating helper. The reply chilled him to the bone, even in the heat of the tropics.

The Sawi, he was told, prided themselves for their hunting and fishing prowess. But there was an even greater expression of manhood. They called it "fattening the pig for the slaughter." It happened when one young man chose to target another young man in this or a neighboring clan, and built a strong web of friendship. The two would hunt together, fish together, roam the forests together, eat together, laugh, and talk together. They became best buddies. Then, when the relationship was secure, the initiator of the friendship would invite his comrade over to his mother's home for a grand meal. During the middle of the feast, when laughter was the language of the hour, and back-slapping good humor seasoned the supper, the first young man would suddenly pull out a long knife, brandish it with delight before the other's face, and when looks of dawning horror increasingly webbed out from the betrayed's eyes, plunge it through his "friend's" chest, piercing his heart.

The mother would come quickly with freshly baked bread that the traitor touched to his dead comrade's genitals before eating it. Then mother and son would open the skull of the victim, scoop out his brains, and consume these as well.

The deadly project was complete: one brave young Sawi warrior had displayed his cunning prowess, and then had ingested all the power of his target. He became a greater man by taking into himself the strength and energy of his betrayed friend.

Don was dumbstruck! How could he communicate the story of Jesus and the love of God to these people if they viewed Judas, the betrayer, as the hero of the tale? And just as important, what was on the tribal menu for supper tonight? Were the Richardsons the next victims of "fattening the pig for the slaughter"? Don slipped out of the men's lodge a wary and troubled man.

### Passion Week Primer

The story has a wonderful ending, which will come at the conclusion of this message. But the central issue for Don and Carol Richardson is one that is key to all that Christians talk about and "celebrate" this week and this day: Why did Jesus have to die? Is his demise at a young age a symbol of weakness rather than strength? Is Christianity a religion of wimps who prided themselves in following the loser rather than the winner? How do you preach Christ on another Good Friday in a world that thrives on war, one-upsmanship, devious politics, profits at all costs, and survival of the fittest in a cosmic game where the rules are heralded every Thursday evening: "outwit, outlast, outplay!"?

Three major families of atonement theory have been proposed over the centuries, to answer such questions. The first is linked to a story Jesus told shortly before this. In Luke 20, as Jesus was wrestling with the leaders, the crowds, and the challenges in Jerusalem during this emotionally charged week of Passover, he told the story we often call the Parable of the Tenants. Jesus said a man planted a vineyard and then turned it over to tenants while he traveled to distant places. The tenants were supposed to look after things for the owner and share with him in the care of the vineyard and its proceeds. But they rebelled and tried to take it all for themselves. They scorned and beat the owner's representatives who came to make reports and collect rent. Then, when the owner sent his own son, confident that the tenants would respect this blood of his blood, they did the unthinkable, killing the heir. They schemed, wrongly, that with the son out of the way, the vineyard would be theirs.

Everyone knew what Jesus was talking about. The vineyard master was God. We humans are the tenants in God's good world. God has sent representatives like prophets to keep in touch, but we reject them. And then, to put things right, God sent his son.

The rest of the drama was about to play out, as Jesus predicted his own death very shortly, just like his parable had anticipated. God has been wronged. God's people have gone the way of wickedness and wastrels. The world is imbalanced, and the Creator isolated from the people who are to him like loved but wayward children.

How will things be made right? Who will bring restoration and renewal and reconciliation? According to the word of the Lord through the prophets, it would happen when God's unique servant entered the picture and rewrote this awful history. It was not clear exactly what the heaven-sent suffering servant would do, but the outcome was sure. After what appeared to be a lackluster residential sojourn, those around the servant would attack him, cause him pain, and kill him cruelly. But when all of those things had happened, there came a new peace between God and humanity, and the former times of alienation were gone.

Anselm interpreted this as Jesus' mission into our world to defend the honor of the Father. Because of the arrogance of spreading sin, and the hubris of human communities that took the image of God which they possessed for rebellious license, the Creator had been shuttered away from the creation, and Yahweh was forgotten except as a curse word.

But along came Jesus. Like one who still remembers the true nature of reality, and appearing in the guise of a humble but faithful servant, Jesus took up the thankless chivalric duty to restore the honor of the king of the castle, the lord of the estate. The Father might have been ready to wipe out the whole of humanity, but then he saw the face of the suffering servant, and realized that this one still held him in honor. The faithful obedience of the one mitigated the divine wrath of God for the many, and life on planet earth was restored and balanced.

Calvin took Anselm's ideas a step further, paying close attention to the forensic language of Paul in Romans and Galatians. It was not merely God's honor that had been violated, Calvin said, but the righteousness of God's justice. We humans were not merely rebellious clods; we had become downright guilty lawbreakers. Before the court of heaven, none could stand with either pride or dignity. The eternal codes of propriety accused every person of failure and transgression and fault.

Enter Jesus. Jesus came as the lawyer for the accused. He did not pretend we were innocent, but openly marked our guilt. Yet when the holy sentence is passed, and capital punishment is ascribed against us, Jesus showed the extent to which he will advocate on our behalf. He himself stepped into the penalty box, he himself climbed up to the gallows, he himself was strapped into the electric chair, he himself received our toxic chemical cocktail, and died our death for us. There is good news about resurrection to come on Easter morning, just as Isaiah hinted at in the closing notes of his lament. But on Good Friday, the good news is that of escape and substitution.

A second family of atonement theories is not the Creator/ Father who needs to take note of Jesus in his sufferings, but we humans. We have forgotten who we are. It may well be that we have offended God, but God is big enough to be able to handle it. What is more important is that we have offended ourselves. We have lost touch with our place in the house of God. We need a high priest who can help us find our way back home.

Jesus did this in a variety of ways. Irenaeus thought that Jesus had to be at least fifty years old when he died, because the point of Jesus' coming to earth was to go through all the stages of human life (fifty was certainly old age at the time) in order to show us how to live and die correctly. We had lost our way. Only when we saw Jesus living our lives out of grace, love, and courage, and even dying well, would we be able to do the same. He called Jesus' work "recapitulation," a replaying of human identity done right. What we observe most of Jesus on this Good Friday is his ability to die with courage and dignity, just as he had lived. When we see Jesus we buck up, and we get our act together, and we recover the best of our humanity.

Of course, later theologians would further emphasize that exemplary character of Jesus' life and death. Abelard saw in Jesus death the power of moral influence. We have grown complacent in our degradation, according to Abelard. Jesus came among us and all we could see was his goody-goody character, and we despised him for it. We taunted him, trying to make him become a normal sinner like the rest of us. We teased him as if he were sub-human. When he refused to play our dirty games we get angry with him, and plot to get rid of him, and ultimately threw him up on a cross in despicable shame. Only when the dastardly deed was done, it was not *he* but *we* who were suddenly cut to the heart. We heard his words from the cross, "Father, forgive them, for they know not what they do!" and we were embarrassed beyond loss of face. We saw in his reflection what we had become, and came to know the ugliness of ourselves for the first time. His morality pierced our immorality and we must turn away. Like the dirty old man in one of O. Henry's stories, the one who saw by lamplight the beautiful woman he once called friend but lost because of the blackness of his own rotten character, then suddenly remembered what he could have been if he had stayed with her instead of becoming his awful self. We turned with him down a dark alley, banged our heads against a wall, and cried out, "Oh God, what have I become?" Still, in Jesus' love we find ourselves anew for the first time.

Schleiermacher and Ritchl took up the same sermon generations later, preaching a morality in Jesus that became an example for us. Jesus' death was not a failure, but the ultimate testimony of love. Did not Jesus himself declare it? "Greater love has no one than this, that a man lay down his life for his friends!" Here was Jesus on the cross, condemned by the political powers of the day for combatting power with love. While all of his troupe could have been sentenced and killed, Jesus was willing to stand along, allowing the others to scurry off to save their skins. But when they later realized what Jesus had done, they gained new courage to be like Jesus as well, and formed a socially-transforming movement that has since spanned the globe. "Be like Jesus!" they declare.

There is also a third approach to atonement theory, and our

gospel reading connects with it. For Luke, God's good world had been plunged into darkness by the viral effects of sin. Creation's brightness had been swallowed up by the shades of evil. Those who were made in the image of God had become ruined, warped, and distorted. It is the scene of Mordred in Tolkien's Middle Earth, where everything once righteous and holy had become twisted, perverted, distressed, and rotten.

All power appeared to be in the hands of the evil one, the "father of lies" as Jesus once called him (John 8:42-47). No relief from the shadows seemed possible until Jesus calmly stepped into the chasm manufactured by iniquity and it closed around him.

Origen called it a ransom to the devil. Satan, he said, was the greatest fisherman of all times, snagging every flipping creature from the waters of this world. When his boat was filled to the limit, he headed for shore and a ravenous meal of consumption that would send us to his infernal bowels forever. But like any good fisherman, the devil snaked a troll line into the boat's wake on the journey back to harbor. Suddenly the reel whizzed out in a furious tug. A giant fish had gone for the devil's spinning lure!

Satan stopped rowing and fought the line. The fish at the other end was huge beyond belief. After playing it with practiced dexterity, the devil finally saw the fish near the gunwales. It was enormous! And, more than that, it was the Creator's own first creation! It was the Son of God!

The devil was in a dilemma. He did not have room for the big fish in his boat. He could keep either his current catch or toss it aside and claim the prize of the day, but he couldn't do both. Like any great fisherman, he chose the record breaker. Shoveling the little fish out of the boat, he managed to tease, taunt, and gaff the big one over the edge, to get it to flop heavily onto the deck. His catch would be the news of heaven and earth!

But as he wrestled his over-committed craft toward the docks, the trophy fish he prized gave a sudden wallop of its mighty tail, capsizing the boat, and escaping into the water. In an instant, the devil was left with nothing.

So, said Origen, is the story of Good Friday, when Satan, the prince of the powers of this age, played his biggest hand, trading all of wicked humankind for the big prize of God's own son, and lost everything in the bargain. Why did Jesus have to die? Because it was the only way to get the rest of us free.

Still, Jesus himself remains in charge of his own existence. And on Easter morning, as we shall soon see, the big fish will get away, as do all of us who swim after him in the waters of baptism.

## Where To From Here?

The story of Jesus' horrible death is as familiar as it is enigmatic. We know that Jesus died, and did so in a cruelly painful way. But the why of it still remains fuzzy. Did Jesus have to satisfy God's honor or justice? Yes, that is indeed a message of the New Testament. Was his death an example to us and an act of moral persuasion? Certainly, for Jesus' own words testified to that. Were the evil powers that have locked their claws into this good creation of God weakened and perhaps ultimately destroyed in Jesus' infamous demise? That, too, is an element of the tale. But all are mixed together in ways that refute easy dissection or quick categorization.

Don and Carol Richardson survived their Sawi sojourn and even succeeded in bringing the gospel to those people. The story that begun above took a later strange turn. Due to increasing scarcity, the Sawi people needed to range further in hunting and fishing. This, in turn, caused them to run into conflict with other nearby tribes and peoples. Soon there were skirmishes and fights and all-out wars. People returned to Sawi homes bloodied, battered, or missing limbs. Sometimes they failed to return at all, claimed by assassins' wounds and swallowed up by the putrefying womb of the jungle.

It was then that the men began to talk openly about the possible need for a "peace child." Intrigued, Don asked what they meant by that term.

Sometimes, they said, when war got too pronounced and murderous, when tribes were in danger of killing one another off, when brutality bested their will to live, one of the chiefs might grab the youngest newborn male baby from its mother's arms, and run swiftly, despite the woman's wailing, across the no-man's-land between the tribes. Reaching the first enemy village, he would thrust the baby into the arms of a young woman.

All knew what this meant. A son from one mother was now the possession of the other tribe. Both tribes had a stake in the child's future, and all warfare would cease for as long as that child lived. The "peace child" reconciled the foes.

With interest mounting, Don asked a further question. What would happen, he queried, if someone should kill the "peace child"? Horrified, the group shook their heads aghast. No one would ever think to do such a dastardly deed. It was beyond belief!

Hmmmm.... thought Don. And then he proceeded. "Let me tell you a story…" he said. And he related a tale of a time when the tribes of heaven and earth were at war with one another. And he told of the chief of heaven bringing his own son across the no-man's-land into our tribe as a "peace child." He explained how one day someone had instigated the murder of that "peace child." When the horrified Sawi warriors begged him about what could be done to erase this monumental human blunder, Don preached Christ, grace, and the forgiving love of God.

That was the day that the Sawi became Christians. Do you understand?

# Night And Light

A friend of mine had rewritten a familiar proverb and used it ominously. "Just remember," he said, "things always look the darkest before the lights go out completely." There was something of that threatening anticipation which always washed over us on this darkening night. We join Jesus and his disciples as dusk falls. They did not know it yet, but within hours the blackness would become very bleak. Jesus would be arrested, they would be scattered, and even Peter would deny and reject his relationship with their very best friend. This was a dark night indeed.

John had prepared us for this. The great transition in John's portrait of Jesus happened between chapters 12 and 13. The first half of the gospel has rightly been called "the book of signs," since it focused on seven specific miracles through which the divine identity of Jesus was increasingly revealed. As the last of these miracles, the raising of Lazarus in chapter 11, was noised about, John told us that "Greeks" came seeking an audience with Jesus (12:21). "Greeks" was a code-term John used for "the world," the larger designation of all peoples on earth, both Gentile and Jews. Remember how Jesus put it in his famous words? "For God so loved *the world* that he gave his only son..." (John 3:16). This was the language of Jews for the rest of humanity. Jesus' signs were done so that the Jews might see, know, and respond to their Messiah. But now, even the Gentiles, the Greeks, the world had observed the light of heaven shining in the darkness and were coming!

## Glory

This is the "hour" of divine revelation! When the "Greeks" came, Jesus knew that the "signs" had accomplished their goal, and the world was looking for its Savior. At this point, Jesus declared that his "hour" had come, the time of the full revelation of his glory that would take place through his passion. The scenes shifted, and John 13-20 became "the book of glory."

Here in John 13, we are told that Jesus knew that his "hour" had come, and so he gathered his disciples for a final meal. Following Mark's lead, the synoptic gospels clearly identified the final meal that Jesus shared with his disciples as a Passover celebration. Yet strangely, for all the other symbolism in the fourth gospel, John clearly steered away from that connection in chapter 13. Why?

The answer appears to have several parts to it. First, John deliberately timed the events of Jesus' final week so that Jesus was tried and sentenced to death on Friday morning (at the same time as the unblemished Passover lambs were being selected), and crucified during the precise hours when the Passover lambs were being slaughtered in the temple courtyard. In this way, John accomplished a purpose that he indicated at the beginning of his gospel, to portray Jesus as the "lamb of God" (1:36). Thus, it was important for John *not* to identify the last supper as the Passover, since Jesus must die with the lambs who were being slaughtered prior to that meal.

Second, this does not immediately mean that either John or the synoptics were telling the story wrong. Instead, there were several different calendars functioning among the Jews of the day, marking the celebration of the Passover with slight variations. These came into being due either to the chronological ordering of each new day (Roman: sunrise to sunrise, or Jewish: sundown to sundown), or the perceived occasion of the new moon that began the month (adjusted differently by Babylonian and Palestinian rabbis).

Thus, Jesus and his disciples probably ate a Passover meal together, as the synoptics identify it, but one which was tied to a different calendar than that used by the bulk of the Jerusalem population. In this way, John could leverage the different schedule to communicate a particular emphasis in his portrayal of Jesus' symbolic identity. Throughout the changes of the gospel, this understanding of Jesus girded everything.

This is why the foot washings took place. The dust of the old expressions of God's activity with these folks was being washed away so that they might travel with Jesus into the new age. And the badge that would mark them would no longer be circumcision but rather a visible expression of love.

### A World Waiting To Be Born

Nevertheless, this intimate gathering of Jesus with his disciples takes place on a very dark night. C. S. Lewis captured well the biblical tension between light and darkness in his space trilogy about Venus. The planet Mars, in his tale, was populated by an ancient race of God's creatures who never gave in to the lure of evil, and remained holy and just. Earth, as we know, it had fallen under the domain of the dark shadows, and the great creator had posted warning signs around it in space. It is off limits to other races, quarantined until the end of time.

Venus, though, is a freshly birthed planet with a more recent "paradise" story of creaturely development. A newly formed pair, similar to Earth's Adam and Eve, danced about in innocent delight.

The evil power in the universe would not allow a divine masterpiece to go long unmarred, however, and he sent a vicious Earth scientist named Weston to introduce sin on Venus by corrupting its lord and lady. In a countermove, the great creator sent an ambassador of his own to Venus. The universe held its breath as the future of this bright world hung in the balance.

Like Adam and Eve at Earth's creation, and like the lord and lady of Venus, we are surrounded by dark powers, yet long for the light of redemption and love. Most of our lives we struggle to see more clearly. But grace breaks through, now and again, in moments of insight and illumination, and those are the moments we have to hang onto. Like a mother who brings a child into this world, God is protective of the lives birthed on planet Earth. When sin stains and decadence destroys, God's first thought is to rescue and redeem and recover the children God so dearly loves.

So darkness threatens, with its denials, betrayals, and broken relationships. I think of Allison and Gary (not their real names), who were high school sweethearts and obviously in love when they first came to talk with me about marriage. Their backgrounds were similar and they had dated for over five years, so they knew each other well. Both families agreed that Allison and Gary were off to a great start.

Three years later they made an appointment with me. Things were a bit rocky in their marriage. Both were faithful to each other, yet each had begun to resent the time the other was spending on outside interests. Gary was into cars and racing; Allison delighted in clothes, work, and friends.

There was a bristling of the air when they talked. Something wasn't right, and they knew it. Allison's mom wanted them to talk with me, since she knew that marriage was for life. The two of them were not as convinced about the permanence of marriage, and both hinted that they might be ready to pack it in.

A year later they were separated. The house was sold. Gary took an apartment and Allison moved back in with her parents. The next year they got a divorce.

What happened? Allison said she always felt as if they were each listening to different music. Gary had the rumbling beat and twang of country in him, and she moved to the provocative drive of rhythm and blues. It was not that they particularly liked those two styles of music; rather, said Allison, it was a sense that each of them was responding to a different note or melody or beat in life. They couldn't get it together.

Eventually both Allison and Gary moved in with other people. Neither married again. Their one attempt at finding "the right one" had convinced them that it would never happen again.

Some marriages go down in a blaze of adultery. So do some testimonies of Christian faith. Most, however, slip away through failed friendships. The bursts of passionate love and emotional testimony slide away as people forget to *live* together. George Santayana put it this way: "He liked to walk alone; she liked to walk alone. So they got married and walked alone together." In the end, that is a recipe for disaster.

# Maundy Thursday

**Love Feast**

And so it plays out on this Maundy Thursday night. The great marriage of Jesus with his disciples is at its brightest. They are basking in "the hour of glory," as Jesus put it. And Jesus is the perfect spouse, honoring his partners, hosting a celebration meal for them.

Still, the darkness threatened, and Judas heard a different love song. Judas slipped out into the night, earbuds catching a different and dark tune.

Peter was almost there with him. "No, Lord!" he said. "You can't wash my feet!" Yet Jesus, the loving partner, went ahead with this most intimate act of devotion.

As the meal continues, Jesus sang the true song of love. This is why we are here tonight. If we want our marriages to last, we need the glue of friendship to make it happen. So, too, in our religion. Do not flirt with the lures and loves songs of this world if you want to stay out of divorce court on judgment day. Do not let the darkness win.

And it will not. Everyone is looking for a new tomorrow, the dawning of justice and mercy embracing, the time of healing and peace.

Easter is just around the corner for us, and in these darkest nights of Holy Week, we need the early morning rays of its promises. I can feel a new tomorrow coming on.

It is night and it is dark. But Jesus is here with us. And regardless of what comes tomorrow, he has a wonderful song of love for us. This is the "hour of glory." This is the night of remembrance. This is the time of the "new commandment" that will keep us humming through the darkness until Easter dawns again ….and again and again.

# Faces At A Funeral

During the nineteenth century, all Oxford graduates were required to translate a portion of the Greek New Testament aloud. Oscar Wilde was assigned this passage from the passion story of Jesus. His translation was fluent and accurate. Satisfied with his skill, the examiners told him he could stop. But he ignored them and continued to translate. Several times more they tried to call a halt to his reading. Finally he looked up and said, "Oh, do let me go on! I want to see how it ends!"

We need to read this story from beginning to end, don't we? In fact, even at the end, when Jesus is on the cross, when Jesus dies his horrible death, we do not want to quit. For the end is not the end, and Easter is just around the corner.

Yet today is Good Friday - or Death Day. Or the day of tragedy. Today we read the story that we do not want to read but we cannot avoid. Today we go to a horrible funeral for someone we know should not be dying or dead.

## Horrible

There was another time when this came home to me. It was a funeral I did not expect with a family I did not know, the aftermath of a tragedy I could not comprehend. Two men drinking at a party, the younger man dating the older man's daughter. A friendly scuffle? Or was it pent-up resentment that never before spied from the shadows? Was it a gun or a mock "shooting match" with scared friends and family? Then was another shot in the barn out back with a smoking weapon in the older man's hand; the younger man dead on the ground.

Someone in our congregation took his friend from work to our worship services. For three months he and his common-law wife and children came on Sunday morning. He told me that he needed God. He told me that he found God at our church. He told me that his life was changing.

He sat steaming in my office. It was his brother that was murdered last night, and he wanted to kill the murderer! First things first, however. I was the only "priest" he knew. Could I officiate at the funeral?

The spattered blood of death became the splattered ink of chatter in our community, gossiped out of every media newsstand. The shooter was a white male, part of a prominent "old" family in our area, a black sheep lingering at the scandalous end of former glory. The dead man swaggered in on another, newer ethnic wave. Hidden behind his charismatic charm was a long record of drugs, theft, drunkenness, and sexual promiscuity.

Of course, the plot thickened. The man with the gun turned out to be brother-in-law to one of my best friends, a member of our congregation and someone I met with monthly in an accountability group. Their stories differed from that of the young brother who asked me to speak at the funeral. My friend and his family emptied their life savings into a fund to buy the best legal counsel for their "obviously innocent" relative. The angry brother, new Christian and newcomer to our worship services, did not know the unspoken protocol of "assigned seating" in our worship space, and had the audacity to plunk his family right in front of the woman whose brother had shot his brother. Now the newcomer worshiped with great urgency of heart, while the couple behind him and his common-law family fumed without worship.

The funeral was horribly difficult. I knew too much and not enough. Where was God in all of this?

When we gathered around the casket in the cemetery, I spoke a few words of committal, offered prayer, and then encouraged the brother to speak. He wept. He moved from shoulder to shoulder, shuddering grief on every neck. As the casket was lowered into the earth, he jumped down on it and blanketed it spread-eagled with his body. He wailed a litany of loss, sorrow, and vengeance that pummeled away any other sound. The world grew chill and still.

Most of the time I am an optimist. I like to think of my outlook as a holy confidence, a trust that God exists and that all things must work together for God's good designs. But sometimes life is not fun, and the events of those horrible weeks linger with me as a shadow not easily erased. This is what the gospel, the horrible good news, reminds us of today.

### Look At The Faces

This is the story that changed everything. It is the longest single episode of Jesus' life that is told by all the gospel writers. While the preaching of the early Christians focused on the amazing event of Jesus' resurrection, no historical event in Jesus' earthly pilgrimage would be more accurately documented than the final night and morning before his crucifixion.

But what happened? What was the impact of these events? How did this one execution become so much more significant than all of the others that crowded the Roman judicial calendar in those months?

For Jerusalem's religious leaders, this was a final breakthrough in the escalating problem of the northern rabbi who was attracting far too much attention. Here was a commoner, a village boy, causing the uneasy civic peace to be disturbed to a point that threatened rebellion and counter-crackdown. Jesus had to be put out of the way, so that normal life, compromised as it was in this Roman occupation, could go on.

For Jesus' own disciples, this day was the beginning of a nightmare. They had traveled with their Master long and far, and they were not ready to fall into this painful pit, abruptly halting the movement that seemed destined for so much more. Suddenly purposeless, they cowered in hidden rooms, challenged at the very thought of appearing in public where their hero had been demonized.

Judas, however, sensed it differently. Had he pushed the envelope and forced Jesus' hand into an armed confrontation with the governing authorities, hoping this would goad Jesus into action and allow them to get on with the business of stirring a popular uprising against the Romans? We can never be sure. But whatever satisfaction he found in bringing his devious plans to fruition, the aftermath turned sour. Rather than lighting a fuse of liberation, the arrest of Jesus had only sunk to a social tragedy. Jesus was dying, and that's exactly where Judas wanted to be as well. After all, the camaraderie of the disciples would never be open to him again. He had been fingered as the traitor and his name would go down in history in infamy.

The Roman soldiers, however, saw nothing more in this crucifixion than another pay day. A shekel a head, or whatever the going rate was, and a little more money to gamble or drink with - the profits of war - the benefits of law enforcement.

Pilate wondered, during this day. He had been troubled when he was forced to get involved in this catastrophe in the making. The high priest should never have sent Jesus his way. There was no good option to this case; every way out was a dishonorable discharge. Even after he publicly washed his hands of the affair, showing his distaste for what was taking place, the matter would not die. Pilate went home to his wife, who then compounded his anxiety when she complained of nightmares about the man he just condemned. Pilate brooded in his chambers. He could not help but think that this haunting was only the beginning of a very deep darkness to come.

But what of the demons and angels? What of God in heaven? What did this event mean to all of them? In the big picture of things, this Friday slipped away almost too quietly, anticlimactically.

### Overhyped?

In essence, nothing happened. The sun came back from hiding, children played in the streets, mothers fed babies, sabbath prayers were chanted, and all fell asleep that night. What had been billed as the showdown of the ages, the ultimate gunfight at OK Corral, the decisive contest at Milvian Bridge, the do-or-die resolution of Marathon, evaporated like a speck of dust flicked from the cuff of trousers — and everyone went home to catch the six o'clock news.

## From Upside Down to Rightside Up

But perhaps that is precisely the point. Life went on. Amazingly so. Life went on. Neither the death squads from hell nor the curse of God from heaven managed to quell life on planet earth. Because Jesus, heaven's own emissary, laid himself like a copper wire across the poles of the seething battery where opposite forces were sparking for battle. And he drained all their energy.

We became the bystander; winners in a conflict focused on us, but resolved by others. Jesus died and the lights went back on in heaven. Jesus died and the lights went out in hell. Jesus died, and "It is finished!" declared the ultimate victory that kept the planets on track in the universe and love still coursing in the veins of women and men made in the image of their Creator. Jesus absorbed, in his death, both the vengefulness of evil and the wrath of heaven, and the outcome was pretty much that life as God intended it went on.

We still live with death and go to our funerals. But they have changed.

A friend called me one Saturday. He was a perennial student, far away from the town that shaped him, and mostly at odds with his family. There was good reason for his mother to chide, nag, and scold, for my friend had lost his faith, and his parents were worried. But the more they pushed the certainty of their beliefs on him, the more he chafed and backed away. He could no longer live in the simplicity of their dogma, even if it gave them shelter and safety.

He wandered in the wilderness of academia, hoping in each class to find a glorious utopia, a grand dream, or at least a tiny map that might point toward some secularized holy grail. Every term he called me to describe his latest faculty mentor, a true savior, finally, who was worthy of his devotion. But this Saturday something was different. There was wistfulness in my friend's voice, and a trembling uncertainty in his words. What if there was no big picture, all-encompassing thesis, or unifying meaning? What if we were tripping with stumbling paces through the wilderness and there was no limit or signpost or way out? What if he was on a quest but there was nothing to find?

"I'm lonely," he told me, and I was left to imagine his cosmic, spiritual aloneness, a void where both heaven and hell were silent and he was left in awful communion with only his inadequate self. There was no dream here, only an incessant heart hunger kept awake by an unrelenting nightmare.

But Jesus' life among us, and his awful, horrible, scandalous, beautiful death somehow bound heaven to earth, God to humanity, eternity to time. We are not forgotten. For the one who thought us into being has become fully a traveler with us. He lived our life — he died our death — and we cannot be forgotten.

### The Funerals Continue

So we go on with our own lives and deaths. My memories of my great-grandmother Bolt are very vague. I was a young lad when my parents took my older sister and me to see her at a retirement home in Willmar, Minnesota. I can remember the strange and mildly irritating smell of the place, and the dim incandescence of the corridor with its waxed linoleum. We tried unsuccessfully to turn down the volume of our clattering steps and shuffled into the room quietly, nervously afraid of arousing death before its time.

"Grandma Bolt" (as we were told to call her) reclined in an oversized lounger, barely aware of us. Her mouth hung open and she wore wrinkled skin several sizes too big over a shrinking frame. A musty afghan draped her carelessly. She couldn't quite catch what my mom tried to tell her in a stage-whisper shout. We touched her hands and she seemed to fumble for ours with gnarled and cold fingers.

I can only recall this single visit to see her, and I know I didn't like it. At the time she was an alien to me, even though I know now that a good deal of her DNA lives on in my own body. When Grandma died my parents didn't take me to the funeral because I was supposedly too young to understand death. Now, some forty years later, I weep inside. I never knew the best of my great-grandma Bolt. I wasn't there when she played as a child with boys like me. I never watched her giggle with friends or flirt with

# From Upside Down to Rightside Up

my great-grandfather. I never experienced the changing moods of her face, a barometer of her passions, fears, and faith. I never heard her sing in church, though I was told she loved the hymns. All I carry with me is the one scary visit of my childhood.

I am old enough now to attend funerals and I have gotten well past my early aversion to assisted care centers. What frightens me these days is the thought that there are probably fewer than 25 people alive today who remember my great-grandmother at all. When we couple dozen die, she will be truly forgotten — a near-century of living, breathing, loving, toiling, memorizing, cooking, knitting, talking, aching, laughing, holding, washing, and befriending vapored and vanished like a six o'clock morning mist.

Nicholas Wolterstorffh reflected on the death of his son with these words: "There's a hole in the world now. In the place where he was, there's now just nothing... There's nobody now who saw just what he saw, knows what he knew, remembers what he remembered, loves what he loved... The world is emptier" (*Lament for a Son*). That's true, as well, of my great-grandmother Bolt. True, too, of a host of good people whose gravestone legacies weather to indecipherable under time's polishing.

It won't be long before I join them, erased from life's hard drive by the re-programmers of a new generation. Some years ago we were comparing ages in our family and one of my daughters remarked to another, "Dad has probably lived more than half his life already." The words shivered through me and robbed me of the fun of the moment. It's true — I have probably lived half my life already. In the not-so-distant future I will be my great-grandmother, and only 25 minds will retain vague images of a wasted has-been.

But Jesus will remember me! Like the thief on the cross, like his mother at his feet, like the disciples cowering in the shadows, Jesus will remember us. Because of Good Friday, he will never leave us. He will never forsake us. He will never forget us.

We are the faces at his funeral. And when it comes time for our own funerals, his face will truly be the only one that matters — for now — for eternity.

# Creation Reborn

When I was a pastor in rural southern Alberta, we held our Easter Sunrise worship services in a cemetery. It was difficult to gather in the dark, since neither mountains nor forests hid the spring-time sun, and the high desert plains lay open to almost ceaselessly unclouded skies. Still, we mumbled in hushed whispers as we acknowledged one another, and saved our booming tones for the final rousing chorus of "Up from the grave he arose…!" We did not shake the earth as much as we hoped. But we were confident that Jesus, who had once laid in a grave, would someday break open these tombs of our friends and family members, and bring in the new creation.

We all ache for resurrection, don't we?! In 1954, Marcelle Maurtette penned his powerful play *Anastasia*. It was based on the true story of a woman named Anna Anderson who claimed to be the long-lost daughter of the last emperor of Russia, Tsar Nicholas II, and his wife, Aleksandra.

The Russian tsars believed their kingdom was imperishable. They knew they would rule forever. But at the turn of the last century, a groundswell of social and political revolution tossed them aside. The emperor and his family were held hostage in the palace and then executed as the Bolsheviks bathed the countryside with blood.

Rumors persisted that little Anastasia, the youngest of the Romanovs, somehow survived the slaughter. Over the years, a number of women claimed to be her. Some were easily spotted as frauds; others convinced enough supporters to make a serious claim to fame.

And then there was Anna—a nameless, homeless, memoryless

wanderer, prone to suicidal fits at the "insane asylum" where she was brought. Nobody knew where she came from. They gave her the name Anna because she had none of her own.

But one day, Anna's doctor came across a picture of the last Russian royal family. Anna bore a striking resemblance to little Anastasia. And she seemed to know more about the Russian noble house than one would expect. Anna was hypnotized, revealing that she knew even more in her subconscious.

There was a real possibility that she could be the only surviving heir of the Romanov family fortune. But who would know for sure? Was there any way to prove it?

Newspapers picked up the story. Was this really Anastasia? By some miracle was her life spared, only to be thrown into this new and dismal tragedy? Or was she only a hoax, a scoundrel, a publicity-seeker? The controversy sold papers, and the press hyped it to the limit.

Enter the old empress. She was not in Russia at the time of the murder of her son and his family, and now she lived in exile. If anyone could know if Anna was truly her granddaughter, this woman would be that person. One day she came to see Anna.

The two women talked together for a long time. When she left, the elderly woman was accosted by reporters, and told the world: "Anna is my granddaughter Anastasia!"

Suddenly Anna began to change. She blossomed as a person. She took hold of her life. The suicide threats were gone. She washed herself and combed her hair. She looked after herself and dressed in style. She stood up straight in a crowd, and she carried herself with dignity when she walked.

One line in the play carried the heart of the story. How did Anna climb from the pit of her insane asylum and walk again in the land of the living? What transformed Anna the nobody into Anastasia the princess? This was her secret: "You must understand that it never mattered whether or not I was a princess. It only matters that ...someone, if it be only one, had held out their arms to welcome me back from death!"

## Recreation

When describing the events of resurrection morning, in that garden cemetery, John gave us some wonderful analogies to see this rebirth happening before our eyes. John was a master of multiple levels of meaning, and we have seen it in his descriptions. For one thing, when Mary looked into the empty tomb, the scene, as John described it, immediately calls to mind the arc of the covenant that symbolized Yahweh's presence in the tabernacle and later the temple. While the other gospel writers told of angels being present, John viewed them through Mary Magdalene's eyes, and saw two such creatures in exactly the same position as the cherubim that stood guard over the mercy seat throne. This time, however, the divine presence was missing, indicating the dawning of a new age in which the Creator's power and presence would not be confined to or limited by a particular geographic location. The second strategy in the divine mission had come, and the gospel was now to be preached to the whole world through Jesus' disciples.

Then, when Mary Magdalene wept because she missed her "Lord" (which is the Greek version of "Yahweh"), a man appeared on her periphery, and she assumed that he was "the gardener." Of course, Mary's perception had to be incorrect, because, as we know from John, the man was actually Jesus. But was Mary really wrong? John never said that Mary was mistaken; only that she had *assumed* he was the gardener. In fact, John appeared to want us, his readers, to get the subtle message that Jesus is *indeed* the gardener. After all, at the beginning of time, the Creator placed Adam and Even in a garden and came to walk and talk with them (Genesis 2). In the re-creation of all things, it is quite appropriate for new life to begin anew in a garden where the great gardener was once again meandering and sharing intimacy with those who were favored friends. John confirmed this symbolic intent when he told us that Jesus said, "Mary." Jesus spoke Mary's name. Just as Adam and Eve, along with all the animals and all elements of creation, came into being when they were named in the first beginning, so now Mary was restored to life in a new way as her identity was regenerated when Jesus spoke her name. The cemetery of the dead among gravestones became the birthplace of new lives and a new creation.

### I Don't Care?

"A grave is a sobering thing," said Wordsworth. We try to mark each with snippets of meaning that will defuse the scandalous superficiality of life that Emily bemoaned in Thornton Wilder's *Our Town*. "If I was so quickly done for," asked the wee voice etched on a child's grave memorial, "what on earth was I begun for?"

Ancient Romans tossed away the scandal of our brief and meaningless lives. When archaeologists first sifted through graveyards of the early centuries of the great Empire, they were caught up short by a plethora of burial plot stones inscribed with the same seven letters: N F F N S N C. These certainly spelled no known Latin word, and other connections escaped would-be interpreters. Until, that is, they uncovered older quadrants of cemeteries where many grave markers carried seven-word inscriptions beginning with these otherwise meaningless letters: *Non Fui. Fui. Non Sum. Non Curo.* Suddenly the intent was clear. So many Romans had found this phrase as the best representation of life and death that even poor people with small stones could abbreviate it down to just seven letters and all would understand: "I was not. I was. I am not. I don't care."

Tragic — cynical — hopeless.

I have officiated at hundreds of funerals over the past 35 years, and never met a family which would have dared place that testimony over the grave of a loved one. We cry. We weep. We wail. One young man even jumped on top of the casket as it was being lowered into the cold earth, pounding in horrible grief on the unforgiving final home of his brother's body.

Even when death is "good," and an elderly grandmother slips willingly from time into eternity, tears of loss trace our cheeks. We were born to live, not to die.

That is why those same archaeologists of ancient Roman artifacts were equally surprised by some of the memorials found next to the burial niches in the catacombs where Christians laid their dead. There were inscribed verses of scripture, to be sure, but also symbols and pictures. The one, however, that mystified most showed the upper body of a man holding a harp. It seemed to represent Jesus, but standard mythological representations usually tied that one to Orpheus.

### The Song Of Orpheus

Orpheus was the darling of Greek love, music, and tragedy. Orpheus was the master musician of his time, and well could have had 39 out of the top forty tunes on the charts at once. When Orpheus sang, the birds swooped in just to flit on his lilting melodies. When Orpheus sang, the clouds rolled back from the skies, the sun shone more brightly, and the beasts crept out of the shadows to dance their fancy footwork. When Orpheus came to town, people floated out of homes and shops to jig in the streets and fall in love.

Of course, when Orpheus himself fell in love, passion intensified. It was Eurydice who caught his eye and heart, and before long they were fawning and fainting after one another. When Orpheus and Eurydice wed, the world shimmered with significance, and couples everywhere twitterpated.

But a week later all meaning was lost. While Eurydice romped with her friends through a field, a snake slithered through the grass and struck her heel. Almost instantly Eurydice was gone, robbed of her nascent marriage and life itself.

Deep in grief, the song died in Orpheus' heart. He only moaned and groaned, and the world hung heavy with pain. Willows drooped their branches in empathy, and the wild beasts slunk back into the shadows. Dark clouds covered the sun's smile, and birds roosted, unable to take flight in the oppressive air.

Orpheus moped and wallowed. Consolation fled. Lament took the orchestra's podium.

Reaching for nerves that rejected grief's cancerous alloy, Orpheus set out on a mission to the undiscovered country. He found the door to the underworld and slid down, down, down, into the kingdom of death. Confronting elusive Hades, Orpheus demanded back the woman he had loved too shortly. Hades would have none of it. His contracts were lethally binding.

Orpheus did what only he could do. He sang a love song. Strumming his harp, Orpheus put his heart to music in a way that sent shivers through the shifting shades and shadows. As his voice reverberated against the wailing walls, one ghost began to thicken and color. A few more stanzas of *amore* and Eurydice stood solid before him once again. They kissed and hugged and held hands all the way to earth's surface, gripped by smiles of incredulous ardor.

### A Christian Orpheus?

The legend of Orpheus grew over time, so that even the most skeptical linked his name to true love. But why would early Christians reconfigure Jesus in the guise of Orpheus? How could they profane the sacred so scandalously?

Obviously, they did not believe in Orpheus. They were martyrs of Christ and traded all trite tales of the marketplace to buy the pearl of great price. Some metaphors command instant understanding, and when these groaning souls recalled the words and deeds of Jesus, it was precisely in the cemetery that conflating Orpheus and Christ made perfect sense.

Christians remembered the day when Jesus traveled to Bethany to mourn his friend Lazarus' death. Jesus should have been there earlier to heal Lazarus of his illness and stay death's untimely call, and everybody knew it. Lazarus' sister Martha came blazing out of the house when she heard that Jesus was approaching. She had sent word of Lazarus' illness to Jesus while there was still time for the great one to make a difference like he did with so many others throughout Palestine. But Jesus had dithered and dallied, and Martha was angry.

"If you had been here, my brother wouldn't have had to die!" she shouted at Jesus. He knew she was right and did not try to defend himself. In great grief, they lumbered slowly to the family home. Professional wailers at the door assaulted their ears, accusing Jesus with fiery eyes. Stooping to enter, Jesus found the other sibling, Mary, covered with torn rags and ashes. "If you had been here, my brother wouldn't have had to die!" she simpered, cutting Jesus deeper than her sister's diatribe.

### A Shepherd's Voice

Jesus cared without self-defense and brought his entourage out to the cemetery. Only a week before he had inspired the Galilee crowds with his delightful homily about shepherds, getting knowing nods about the nasty hirelings who lead sheep astray and bring them into the fold of death - the worst shepherd of all. Leaning on the best of Israelite heritage, Jesus mounted the shoulders of shepherd boy/King David, and reclaimed the dignity of the office Ezekiel celebrated in chapter 34 of his prophecy. Jesus said his sheep knew his voice and would follow him anywhere. He also mentioned, cryptically, that he had other sheep, not of the flock in front of him, and that he had to go and call them.

The disciples must have thought about these things as they now stood with Jesus in the local cemetery. He challenged the keepers of the place, demanding that they roll back the stone covering the carved cavern where Lazarus' body had been laid, allowing the maggots to do their work. The cemetery tenders shook their heads. "You don't want to do that," they replied. "He stinks!"

But Jesus repeated his request with demanding authority and the workers shrugged. When the grave yawned, it burped death's stench. Only Jesus did not cringe and retreat. Standing resolutely in the land of the living, he cried out with the voice of the good shepherd to his friend now taken captive in death's dark fold: "Lazarus!" And down, down, down, in the depths of the netherworld, owned by that worst of the bad shepherds, death itself, Lazarus heard his Master's voice, and came through the dark window of the grave to stand once again in the sun next to his shepherd.

### Easter Testimony

This is why the Christians in Rome conflated the myth of Orpheus with the reality of Jesus. They did not trust in human legends. But they did hang their hopes on the one who said to Martha and Mary, "I am the resurrection and the life!" and then proved it that day in Bethany. In fact, the Roman Christians knew that Jesus had confirmed all of this a short while after the incidents of John 10-11, when he himself went down, down, down, into the depth of death, and came up again on Easter morning as the Lord of life.

And, as wives bade farewell to husbands who had been torn apart by the beasts in the coliseum, as children wrapped the bodies of parents in burial clothes, as friends mourned the deaths of their kindred spirits, the great metaphor of Jesus as the true Orpheus told the most magnificent promise of all. For even in these dark days of deathly haunts, followers of Jesus knew that one time soon the good and great shepherd would shout the names of their loved ones down to Hades itself, and even though captured in shepherd death's lockdown fold, their family and friends would hear their Master's voice, and they would rise to life and follow him into the eternal kingdom.

We all try to evade and fool death, stymying him with tummy tucks and fleeing him through our exercise routines and vitamins. But come death shall, with fateful inclusiveness, whispering our names at night or noon, and, against our wheedling and pleading, will march us into his awful gloom. Then the hope of our faith will endure its final test. For if the gospel is true, our good, great, and chief shepherd will not forget us, but will march down, down, down, to Sheol and sing us his song of love. And we, who know the voice of our Master, with rise into the dawn of eternity and follow the one who calls us by name.

# Messiah's Community

In his widely-read testimony, *Man's Search for Meaning,* famed psychiatrist Viktor Frankl remembered a terrible day during World War II. He was on a work gang, just outside the fences that hid the horrors of Hitler's infamous Dachau death camp. "We were at work in a trench," wrote Frankl. "The dawn was gray around us; gray was the sky above; gray the snow in the pale light of dawn; gray rags in which my fellow prisoners were clad, and gray their faces."

Frankl told how he was ready to die. It was as if the gray bleakness had claws, and each moment they dug deeper and colder into his soul. Why go on? What could be the purpose in "living" if, indeed, he was even still alive at this moment? There was no heaven, no hell, no future, and no past. Only the clutching grayness of this miserable moment.

Suddenly, to his surprise, Frankl felt "a last violent protest" surging within himself. He sensed that even though his body had given up and his mind had accepted defeat, his inner spirit was taking flight. It was searching. It was looking. It was scanning the eternal horizons for the faintest glimmer that said his fleeting life had some divine purpose. It was looking for God.

In a single instant two things happened, says Frankl, that simply could not be mere coincidence. Within, he heard a powerful cry, piercing the gloom, and tearing at the icy claws of death. The voice shouted "yes!" against the "no" of defeat and the gray "I don't know" of the moment.

At that exact second, "a light was lit in a distant farmhouse." Like a beacon it called attention to itself. It spoke of life and warmth and family and love. Frankl said that in that moment he began to believe. And in that moment, he began to live again.

### "And He Breathed Into Them The Breath Of Life..."

This was the moment, in a different time and context, that we read about today. Jesus had risen from the dead, but that kind of strange thing cannot easily be believed. The disciples still lived in darkness. They still doubted, wondered, and could not wrap their minds around all of the craziness that was taking place, plus the strange stories their friends were telling.

Suddenly Jesus appeared, a glow of light in the middle of their dark doubts and fears. Then Jesus did something strange. John told us that he "breathed on them" (20:21), imparting to his disciples the divine Spirit, and sending them out as his ambassadors, exactly in the manner of which he prayed back in chapter 17, on Thursday night, before the betrayal, arrest, farce of a trial, and horror of crucifixion. Is this, as some have suggested, John's different version of Pentecost (Acts 2)?

Actually no, it is not. John was very consistent about every detail in his gospel. Remember that on Thursday night, as they sat together in the upper room, eating a meal, Jesus had a lot to say. He told his disciples that they would run from him. He said that he was leaving them. He made it clear that they would be frightened and discouraged, and that the world would threaten them.

But he also said that he would send to them the "Paraclete." The Holy Spirit, the "Comforter." When Jesus left the disciples to return to glory, the Holy Spirit would continue to connect them with each other. It would be like heaven's Wi-fi system, present everywhere. The Holy Spirit would keep them connected to Jesus.

### Living Witnesses

In a sense, this was a final expression of the re-creation process that highlighted John's gospel. Just as Adam only came alive to his life and livelihood at the beginning of time when God breathed into him the divine breath (Genesis 2), so now this tiny gathering of the new humanity could not function until they were divinely enthused in a similar, very literal manner. The

Creator who breathed the breath of life into Adam in the first creation breathed the same breath of life into his disciples in this re-creation. The dead of the world were coming back to life!

John ended his gospel with the story of Thomas, who demanded the proof of physical evidence in order to believe this good news. "My Lord and my God!" Thomas exclaimed (20:28). With these words, John finalized the link between the man Jesus and the deity worshiped by Israel in the Old Testament. Though John never gave a nativity story in which Jesus' miraculous birth was told, here he announced the full and complete incarnation, Jesus was both human (he had physical wounds) and divine (he was worshiped in a manner reserved otherwise only for Yahweh). Thus, Jesus was and is the true Messiah of Israel.

Although Jesus provided Thomas' requested touch, Jesus commended those others who could become reborn human creatures through faith that was not dependent upon direct experiential contact with Jesus' physical body. In this, the missionary nature of John's gospel message was affirmed, for John ended by issuing an invitation to the same trust and belief to all who read it (20:30–31), even though they do not have opportunity to touch the physical features of Jesus.

John is picturing the Body of Christ being birthed. Creation happened at the beginning of time. But the deadly virus of evil penetrated God's good world. Darkness washed over everything until life seemed gone forever. But now, through Jesus, creation was being reborn. Jesus was the light of the world. Jesus was the light that gave life to all things. And here, in the darkness of this shadowed room, Jesus breathed the Holy Spirit into the disciples, and they rose up the living Body of Christ.

Paul S. Minear served us well when he penned his famous study years ago, *Images of the Church in the New Testament*. After identifying a variety of what he termed "minor images," such as "salt," "letter," "fish," "boat," "net," "loaf," and a dozen or so more, Minear went on to focus a chapter each on the "major images" of "People of God," "New Creation," and "Fellowship in the Faith." But all of these were still preliminary to the towering image that drew the rest into itself. If there is one idea about the church in the New Testament, said Minear, that captures the essence of every nod and note and nudge in its direction, it is the grandiloquent concept of "Body of Christ." Here the rest of the images come together and make sense. Here the whole becomes larger than the parts and inanimate theology puts on flesh and moves.

The body image affirms individuality, while it pulls everyone up into community. There is both independence of self and dependence of organism that stream together into a more comprehensive interdependence. Moreover, the head remains that of Christ, giving shape to the rest of the being as a reflection of divine intentions and purposes. Few theological descriptions are as pervasively significant and as inherently usable as that of the church as the Body of Christ.

### Knit Together

Perhaps the greatest expression of what the Body of Christ means is community. In his book on civility, *A World Waiting to Be Born*, M. Scott Peck mused that community was lacking in our world and hard to recover. Perhaps, because of the time that we are forced to spend with one another at work, we might bring about a little of it there, he said. Maybe even in marriages and families, if we count the true cost of divorce. But Peck was quite certain that community could never happen in churches. After all, he said, community requires that we spend time together and that we choose to work through our differences with one another. But church life in North America, according to Peck, had become another consumerist enterprise with little corners of the Sunday cafeteria serving up differing musical and message morsels to taste, and Christians grazing briefly in politeness before they re-isolated themselves from the threat of community.

This is a harsh assessment, isn't it? Unfortunately, we fear it might be true. We may be card-holding members of the same congregations, but we are too often not on the same page with one another. Politics divide us. Socio-economic situations separate us. Races split in the church as well as elsewhere in society.

Somehow the one Holy Spirit of Jesus does not seem to breathe the same way in all of us.

One of M. Scott Peck's earlier books, *The Different Drum*, analyzed community and how it evolved. There are four stages to developing deep community, according to Peck: pseudo community, conflict, chaos, and true community. The first is our surface friendliness in group settings because we are nice people. Most churches are probably at least an expression of this. But bring any conflict, and tensions flare. At this point, according to Peck, we have the options of staying together and working things through or going our separate ways. God and the Bible point in the former direction, but our experientialist society mostly pushes us the other way, because we want pleasure, not pain.

The committed few who grapple with conflict and come out the other side often suddenly experience chaos. We've stayed together, but what's the point? Who's in charge around here anyway? Who will validate our raggedy band? And without clear lines of authority or comforting leadership, too often "things fall apart," as Yeats said in his famous poem, "The Second Coming", and Achebe diagrammed in his 1958 novel, *Things Fall Apart*.

But if community is a divine gift, something profoundly wonderful can happen to and for those who cling to it, hope, and pray. This beautiful outcome is the church, the Body of Christ, the family of faith, the people of God, the year of jubilee in all of its fullness.

### Messiah's Community

One of my favorite stories about community comes from eastern Europe. In a small town on the edge of a large forest, the main worship center was a Jewish synagogue. Just outside the town stood a monastery, old and run-down, with only five brothers still puttering around grounds too extensive for them to care for.

It had been a great spiritual center at one time, with dozens, sometimes hundred, of monks, seekers, and spiritual men. But that was long ago. The abbot wondered what would happen if another monk died. There seemed to be no meaningful future for the few who remained. Not only that, but these were folks who were not growing old gracefully. When they went into town for supplies, the local shopkeepers sighed. The guys were grouchy and complained about everything. They wanted discounts the sellers could not afford. They expected special treatment, since they were "men of God." Nobody liked them.

The congregation at the synagogue was aging and shrinking as well. Young people went to the cities for work or school, and they did not come back. The young families became middle-aged, and the middle-agers retired, got old, and died. Two dying communities. Perhaps it was their precarious outlooks that brought the rabbi and abbot together. Over time, they became friends, in part because they seemed to be the final leaders of end-of-life spiritual centers.

Each Friday, before Shabbat began, the rabbi and the abbot would walk for a while in the woods. They would laugh. They would feel the cool breezes and enjoy the songs of the birds.They would also commiserate about the people under their care.

One Friday, when the abbot got to the forest, the rabbi was waiting for him, and rather impatiently. "I have to tell you something," said the rabbi in nervous and excited tones. "I don't know really how to say it, but here goes. Last night, the Holy One (blessed be his name) came to me in a vision. He said to me, 'I want you to give a message to the abbot when you meet him tomorrow. I want you to tell him that one of the brothers is the Messiah.'"

The abbot was dumbfounded. So was the rabbi. The whole vision thing made no sense. For one thing, the rabbi was sure that when Messiah came, he would be a Jew. Certainly, Messiah would not be one of the cantankerous old guys at the monastery. Similar thoughts flowed through the abbot's mind. He had been worshiping Jesus all his life. Jesus was the Messiah, and none of the men at the monastery was Jesus. This was strange. This was ludicrous. What was going on? The rabbi swore he had seen the vision and that it was true. But how could it be?

When the abbot and the rabbi parted ways after their walk,

they were no longer talking. Both were troubled and concerned. Each believed God could speak in visions and dreams. But why this vision? And why bring it to the rabbi instead communicating directly to the abbot? Nothing about this made sense.

The rabbi headed back to the monastery. That evening, when the brothers were gathered for dinner, he decided to tell them about it. "The rabbi told me something very strange today," he said. "The rabbi had a vision last night. God came to him and commanded him to tell me that one of us here, at the monastery, is Messiah!"

All four brothers stopped eating in mid-bite. All turned to stare at the abbot. No one moved or said anything for a long moment.

Then they began to chuckle — and laugh — great belly laughs. Soon they were in tears with hilarity.

When they returned to their small rooms for evening personal devotions, everyone was in a good mood. Chuckle medicine had lifted their spirits.

But then the wondering began. Certainly, the rabbi was wrong. Certainly, Messiah had come long ago. Certainly, none among them was Messiah come again. Of course not!

Yet, what if it were to happen like that? What if Messiah decided to come to earth again? Would Messiah show up here? Could Messiah be found in this place, among these brothers?

The nagging obsessions lingered. It was not the case, of course, but if, *if* Messiah was to be one among them, who might it be?

Certainly, the rabbi himself would be a good choice. He was, after all, their leader, and their spiritual director. Maybe...

What about Brother Elred? He did not speak much, hardly ever said anything to anyone. But when he sang, it was like the voice of an angel! His face glowed, and all heaven shone around him!

Could it be Brother John? Yes, he was gruff. But he was also kind. Would give you the shirt off his back. He helped everyone anytime.

And what about Brother Joseph...? The musing and the

mulling continued long into the darkness.

When dawn broke the next day, the brothers gathered, as usual, for morning prayers. They all looked the same, but it was actually a new group of people. Something happened during the night, and each was now a bit of a different person. Nobody said anything about it, but they began to treat one another with greater kindness. Cross stares and gruffness were gone. There was more smiling, more laughter. Work was finished more quickly and with less complaining.

Even the people in town noticed the change. Shopkeepers no longer feared having the brothers around. In fact, on weekends, some families would pack picnic lunches and head out to the monastery lawns, hoping a brother might come over an join them. Sometimes a brother would sing a song with a child. Sometimes a mother would ask him to pray for her family.

Then, one night, two young men knocked at the abbot's door. They had been traveling for days, they said. The reputation of this place was wafting out. People knew that these were spiritual men, close to God, strong in faith. The young men wanted to live for a while at the monastery and find out whether they were called to ministry.

Others trickled in, and then the guests, spiritual apprentices, and monks-in-training multiplied. Soon they had to repair old buildings and build new accommodations. Eventually they pushed back the boundaries of the place and reworked the entrance and road in. Some enterprising monks crafted a large arch that welcomed people to this place of grace. It had two words on it: "Messiah's Community."

No one ever identified which among the original five brothers was Messiah. In fact, it did not matter. For when they remembered who they were, when they reconnected with Jesus by the Holy Spirit, Messiah lived in and through all of them.

And everyone knew it.

# Starting Over

Sometimes the healing of our hurts starts only when we find another song to sing. Take the story of Helen, for instance. She had her sights set on a law degree from Ohio Wesleyan College. But then the flu epidemic of 1918 hit, taking her father as a victim. Suddenly everything had changed. Helen could not go to college; she had to get a job to support her mother.

For the next ten years, Helen worked at an electrical utility; a simple, repetitive cog in the company machine. Just when she thought she was destined to remain lonely and unmarried, young Franklin Rice stepped in. He was a dashing entrepreneur, an up-and-coming banker. When they married in 1928, Helen's future was bright with promise.

A year later, though, the stock market crashed, and Franklin's financial world fell apart. He could not take the pressure, so he committed suicide. The litany of Helen's life had become an unrelenting nightmare of overwhelming: a deceased father, a lost career, a vanished fortune, a dead husband, and a lonely existence.

Still, more people know Helen than we might think. You see, Helen eventually took a job with the Gibson Greeting Card company. As she began to write the verses for card, people began to realize how much she was able to articulate the thoughts of their hearts and the passions of their souls. It was during these creative days that Helen Steiner Rice became a folk poet who spoke the language of thousands of Christians.

Some years ago, Helen was asked which poem she thought was her best. She hesitated for a moment. She could not tell, she said. Then she went on. There was one that had meant the most to her, ever since the words tumbled out. It was this verse:

*So together we stand at life's crossroads*
*And view what we think is the end.*
*But God has a much bigger vision*
*And he tells us it's only a bend.*
*For the road goes on and is smoother,*
*And the pause in the song is a rest.*
*And the part that's unsung and unfinished*
*Is the sweetest and richest and best.*
*So rest and relax and grow stronger.*
*Let go and let God share your load.*
*Your work is not finished or ended;*
*You've just come to a bend in the road.*

(in the public domain)

Powerful! And we all know what she is talking about, don't we?!

### After Good Friday

I think of Helen's story and the insight of her poem when I read this last chapter of John's gospel. The disciples had been displaced from their homes and careers. For a while, they experienced the exhilaration of being "married" to Jesus, sharing a life that was no less than bringing the kingdom of heaven to earth. They walked in humble pride next to their wise and miracle-working leader.

But then things were catastrophically upended. Jesus was ripped away from them, shamefully treated and torturously executed. So now they were cautious. They were tenuous — hoping, but fearing. Jesus came back to them, to be sure, but all was not the same. Jesus was not the same. And their daunting mission of revolution had less clarity than it did before. What kind of revolution? What kind of kingdom? And would Jesus even stick around long enough for them to find out?

"I'm going fishing," Peter said. What else was there to do? So they all stumbled down to the sea, and numbly went through the motions they learned as lads.

No fish that night. But that was really not the point of coming out there anyway. The men needed to do something routine and ordinary. They needed to live again.

Then, out of the darkness, shined Jesus. They wondered at first, nervous about the shimmering ghost on the shore. But his voice steadied them, and his command strengthened them. All at once they were wildly successful fishermen. The net could hardly hold their enormous draught.

Yet it was not the fish that excited them. Nor did they conceive of themselves as successful lords of the sea. Instead, they were drawn to Jesus. They needed to be with Jesus.

It is fascinating to note that the gospel of John is actually quite complete at the end of chapter 20. Although no manuscripts exist of the book, excluding chapter 21, which is viewed as a later appendage. Still, even if it was written later by the evangelist or one of his disciples, the story it tells brings further completeness to the rest of the gospel.

### Living Into Easter

For one thing, it sets the mission of the church in motion. In John 20, Jesus breathed the Holy Spirit into this new body of his that recreated the human race, like the divine creative story in Genesis 2. Yet these new living souls did not set out immediately on the campaign of resurrected life before that chapter closed. There was intent; Thomas' great testimony was a prelude to all the other testimonies of faith that would be given, but it did not lead naturally or directly into them. Here in John 21, the story of the church began to roll forward. The disciples needed to make choices about their futures, Jesus restored Peter to his leadership role in the enterprise, and the Lord of life articulated a vision about the future that would lead them on.

Secondly, the failures of Peter, so pronounced in the passion story, were rectified. Peter was resurrected by the resurrected Jesus and re-empowered to take initiative again. Yes, he was a good fisherman, and this was a noble calling in life. But he had been transformed by Jesus to a new career, one that involved tossing his nets into an even greater sea.

Third, the missionary character of John's gospel is re-

# From Upside Down to Rightside Up

invigorated by the story of this morning meal on the beach. The prologue to the gospel makes the whole story of Jesus a divine missionary enterprise: Jesus is the word, the light penetrating the blackness of our world, the radiance of almighty God. But that blaze of glory was veiled for a time as those around Jesus wrestled with his identity. Then the miracle of Easter happened, and, for a time, the disciples wrestled with the meaning of all those things. Now, finally, questions of Jesus' identity could be set aside. He is risen! He is Lord! He is all powerful! So it was time to get back to the mission. While Jesus was heaven's bright light, he was laser-focused and limited by his physical limitations. Only when the disciples began to glow could the light be spread, and the mission recovered. John's gospel was all about "light" and "darkness." Here, after a night in the darkness of night that proved unprofitable and seemingly wasted, they were brought into the light of glowing campfire as dawn was breaking, and they were given a new purpose. They were able to start over. Jesus, who was and is the vision of heaven, became their vision here on earth. The church was born.

Centuries ago, the great theologian Cyprian said that a person who has God as his father, has the church as his mother. Why? Because the church was the means by which God strengthened, deepened, and restored our faith. We learn of God from the psalms, hymns, and spiritual songs of the church. We see God in the testimonies of the saints. When we've lost our way, the church directs us to the one who lives within her and draws us back to him. At the heart of the church is Jesus, head of the body.

It is a bit like the experience columnist Robert Fulghum wrote about years ago. He said that long before he had given up any significant relationship with God. He didn't really want God, the church, or religion to cramp his style.

Then he met someone who prevented him from banishing God from his life. He was so amazed that he put her picture on the mirror above the sink where he washed each morning. Every time he cleansed his hands, she was there to cleanse his heart. Whenever he scrubbed his face, she was there to wash his soul.

94

He met her in Oslo, Norway, during the Nobel prize ceremonies one year. He was standing among the crowd of guests that filled the doors and hallways of the auditorium.

Then she passed by. She stopped for a moment and smiled at him. For a brief moment, it seemed as if she had reached into his heart and understood him. There was no condemnation in her look, only genuine care. Then she went to the front of the auditorium to receive the Nobel Peace Prize from the hand of the king of Norway. It was Mother Teresa of Calcutta.

Somehow, said Fulghum, she reminded him of the things that were missing in his life. "We can do no great things," she said, "only small things with great love." With that, wrote Fulghum, "she upsets me, disturbs me, shames me. What does she have that I do not?"

But deep inside, he knew. That's why he kept her picture on his mirror and looked into her eyes again and again. That's why he wrote about her. He knew that she had God. That was the source of her strength, her energy, and her inner beauty.

But Mother Teresa was herself only a reflection of the one who first gave her a vision as well. Like the disciples at the seashore, in the initial encounter, we all need to see Jesus. And when we see him, we can start life again — with purpose — with mission with passion.

### Reborn

A.J. Cronin was a doctor who worked in England in the 1920s, and saw this well. In his autobiography, *Adventures in Two Worlds*, he described working in the hospital of a poor northern mining district early in his career.

One evening a boy dying of diphtheria was brought to him. The hospital was dirty and poorly equipped, with no trained help. Still, Cronin had no alternative but to cut a hole in the boy's throat and insert a breathing tube in his windpipe. Only this emergency tracheotomy saved the fellow's life.

Exhausted, Dr. Cronin left the room. He called a young nurse to sit by the bed. She was only a wisp of a girl, and half starved, but she was a nurse, and she would have to do. "Make sure the tube stays clear, and don't take your eyes off of him," he told her. Then he lay down in a corner and slept.

Suddenly the young nurse was shaking him. She had fallen asleep too, and the tube had shifted. The boy had suffocated; he was dead.

Dr. Cronin's eyes blazed in anger. He told her that he would report her, that she'd never work as a nurse again. Standing in front of him, frail, timid, and shaking like a leaf, she mumbled something under her breath. "What's that you're saying?" he demanded.

So she said it a little louder: "Please give me another chance!" But he was furious that she dared ask such a thing. "You're finished," he said. "There will be no more chances for you!"

He stormed away and tried to sleep. But sleep wouldn't come because her words echoed through his mind: "Give me another chance. Please, give me another chance!"

In the morning he tried to write the letter of discipline, but the picture of her pleading face wouldn't leave him. Finally, he tore the letter up.

But that was not the end of the story. That poor, feeble creature, more child than woman, went on to become the matron of one of England's greatest children's hospitals. In her later years, she was known throughout the nation for her wisdom and devotion.

You see, she never forgot what happened that night. She never forgot her failure; but neither did she forget the grace that had given her a second chance. She carved her future out of her past, based upon one slim vision of eternity. She saw a new future. God's future. And she became part of it.

# Hearing A Familiar Voice

As parents of three wonderful daughters, my wife and I can sympathize with the couple who sent their child off to college, only to find out a few months later that she was dating another student, and that the two of them were already talking about marriage. The troubled parents urged their daughter to bring her boyfriend home so that they could meet him. When the college twosome arrived and hurried and worried greetings were made at the door, Mom shunted daughter off to the kitchen while Dad guided the boy firmly into the family room for a little heart-to-heart.

"So," Dad said at last, trying to find out more about this young man, "what are your plans for your future?"

"I'm not sure, sir," the boyfriend replied, "but I know that your daughter and I were destined to be together, and that God will provide."

"Well, what about finances? How do you intend to pay the bills if you should get married?"

"To tell you the truth, sir, we haven't given that much thought yet. But we are deeply in love, and we are confident that God will provide."

This was not giving the father much confidence, so he pressed on. "Do you have any ideas about careers and where you will live, and whether you will both finish college?"

"We're planning to take it one day at a time, sir," came the reply, "and we're sure that God will provide."

Later that night Mom and Dad were finally alone together, and she said to him, "Well, what do you think?"

"I have mixed feelings," he told her. "On the one hand, the

fellow seems to be a deluded, shiftless, irresponsible fool who hasn't even begun to understand how life works. Yet on the other hand, I get the sense that he thinks I am God!"

## Cryptic

Most of us will never be confused with God, will we? But Jesus certainly had that problem. And, for good reason: he was God!

Of course, that is so unexpected. Good religious folk in Jesus' day already had a relationship with God. They knew of God. They knew about God. They worshiped God.

At the same time, they were strangely attracted to Jesus. And some said that he was God. But that could not be. Everybody had an opinion about Jesus. Still, it was all so confusing. So the religious leaders came to him to ask him straight out: "Are you the Messiah?" Are you the representative of God? Are you God come among us?

And Jesus gave them directly indirect answers. It is a bit like this: if you know me, you know me; if you do not, you do not. Is that fair? Is that clear? What exactly had Jesus meant?

I think it has to do with something that George Herbert wrote in one of his perceptive poems. Generations ago Herbert penned a brilliant picture of the aching in each of our souls. It was called "The Pulley," and in it Herbert portrayed God at the moment of creation, sprinkling his new human creature with treasures kept in a jar beside him. These were God's finest resources, given now as gifts to the crown of his universe: beauty, wisdom, honor, pleasure… All were scattered liberally in the genetic recipe of our kind.

When the jar of God's treasures was nearly empty, wrote Herbert, God put the lid on it. The angels were surprised. They wondered why God did not finish the human concoction, having left this one great resource still in its container. What was left behind, God told the angels, is "rest." God chose not to grant that divine treasure to the human race.

The angels, of course, asked why. Herbert was ready with the divine answer regarding the best mix for the human spirit. humankind, said God, would be rich with gifts and talents beyond measure. But people would also remain restless, searching for something more, wishing for things transcendent, reaching for the stars or heaven or whatever might be out there.

Only if the mighty human race, with all its immense capabilities and capacities, remained restless would it eventually seek its way back to its Creator. Herbert saw well that the strong talents and marvelous abilities of humankind would make us like impatient children, eager to strike out on our own and find our self-made destinies. Only if God would hold back a sense of full satisfaction from our souls would we search our way back home.

This remains a perennial theological paradox: it is the creative act of God that gives us freedom. Yet when we use our abilities for our own ends, we tend to lose what is best in ourselves and often demean it in others, pushing like adolescents away from our spiritual parent. Only if we become restless to find the face of God in some longing for home will we regain a glimpse of our own best faces reflected back toward us in the kindness and smile of God.

This is what Jesus meant when he told the crowds, "My sheep listen to my voice..." If the restlessness of divine urgency causes our hearts to seek God, we know who Jesus is.

### "His Master's Voice..."

Remember that great advertising slogan of RCA Victor? A dog sat looking at the amplification horn of a gramophone. The caption underneath said, "Hearing his master's voice." Whimsical, to be sure. But also touching. To have that sense, even if we cannot see our Master, that his voice is audible, his presence is near, his care is always certain.

One writer told of attending a business conference where awards were being given for outstanding achievements during the past fiscal year. A woman was called to the podium to receive the company's top honor. Clutching her trophy, she beamed out at the crowd of over 3,000 people. Yet in that moment of triumph, she had eyes for only one person. She looked directly at her supervisor, a woman named Joan.

The award-winner told of the difficult times that she had gone through only a few years earlier. She had experienced personal problems, and, for a time her work had suffered. Some people turned away from her, counting it a liability to be seen with her. Others wrote her off as a loser in the company. The worst part was that she felt they were right. She had stopped at Joan's desk several times with a letter of resignation in her hand. She knew she was a failure.

But Joan said, "Let's just wait a little bit longer." And Joan said, "Give it one more try." And Joan said, "I never would have hired you if I didn't think you could handle it!"

The woman's voice broke. Tears streamed down her cheeks as she softly said, "Joan believed in me more than I believed in myself!"

Isn't that the message of the gospel? Isn't that the story of the Bible? That God believed in us while we were still sinners, while we were still failures, while we were at the point in our lives that we could not seem to make it on our own?

That is why Jesus came. And those who know it, hear his voice. He does not need to explain himself to them. Meanwhile, those who know God but do not truly need God, have a difficult time understanding who Jesus is and was.

Thomas Merton, when writing about the religious community with which he spent many years, noted that every prospective participant was initially brought in and made to stand in the center of a circle formed by current members. There he was asked by the abbot, "What do you come seeking?"

The answers varied, of course, in line with the individual's recent experiences. Some said, "I come seeking a deeper relationship with God." Others were more pragmatic: "I desire to become more disciplined in my practices of life." And there were always a few who were simply running away: "I hope to find solace from the world and refuge from the problems that have plagued me."

But Merton said that there was really only one answer which all needed to voice before they could take up residence. "I need mercy!" was the true cry of the heart. "I need mercy!"

Merton said that any other answer betrayed our prideful assertion of self-determination. We wanted, we planned, we were running away from, we desired... But the person who knew his need of mercy had stepped out of the myopic circle of self-interest long enough to begin to see the fragile interdependence of all who were taken into the larger fellowship of faith.

"My sheep listen to my voice..." said Jesus. Can you hear him?

# The Accent Of Heaven

She opened our eyes to the way that civilizations unfold and develop. Cultural anthropologist Margaret Mead became the talk of society with her study, *Coming of Age in Samoa*. For decades she toured the world, explaining what she had observed as children were born, how they were raised, what families and groups did to reinforce certain behaviors, what happened to non-conformists, what marriage looked like, and how people aged and died.

When Ms. Mead was speaking at a university, one student asked her what she considered to be the first sign of civilization in any given culture. This was a good question, with a number of different possible responses. Was cultivation of nutritious plants the first sign of civilization? How about the domestication of some species of animals? Maybe it was the creation of cooking or storage pots? Perhaps it was the crafting of spears, fishing tools, and arrowheads?

But Ms. Mead's answer surprised everyone. She said that the first sign of civilization was represented, in her mind, by a healed femur.

A healed femur? Of course, most immediately wondered what a femur was. The femur is the human thighbone, the main body support of the leg.

But why was this a sign of civilization? At the look of uncertain stares, Ms. Mead went on to explain.

The law of the jungle, she said, is this: "You fall, you die!" If a large predatory animal chases you, only running, jumping or climbing might save you. But if you step into a hole and fall and break your femur, you cannot get up or run or climb to safety. If you fight an enemy and your femur is broken, you cannot crawl away to find water or food. In the jungle before civilization, broken femurs never get healed. Instead, those who break that bone die quickly. On their own, no one ever survives a broken leg long enough to have the bone heal.

For that reason, said Ms. Mead, when we uncover a human skeleton and find a healed femur, we know that someone was there to care about this person. What this person could not do on her own, on his own, someone else did for them. Someone chased away the charging beasts. Someone fought off the predator and the enemy. Some kept watch through the night hours, providing safety. Someone foraged for berries and fruit enough to feed two people. Someone got water and brought it to the person who fell. Someone, at great expense to her own life, dragged this crippled fellow to a place of safety, lit a fire, kept watch, brought food, and stood guard for weeks, while the other healed.

"This is the first sign of civilization," said Ms. Mead. There was not a dry eye in the auditorium. Everyone knew she was right.

True civility, genuine community, honest care, and love are all deeply related. This is why Jesus spoke "a new command" to his disciples on the eve of his death. John gave us the story of Jesus' life and ministry as a tale of re-creation. Remember? He started out the gospel mimicking Genesis 1: "In the beginning..." He talked about the original creation, and how it began to die because of sin. He told us that God decided to re-create this world without destroying humankind. John pointed to Jesus as the living and creative word, from the Genesis account of beginnings, who now entered human society in the middle of time as the word and light bringing restoration and life.

The story of Jesus was and is the story of re-creation. The life of Jesus was and is a documentary about getting back to being human in the way that God intended for us. And the disciples of Jesus were the beginning of a new civilization where femurs could be healed, because these children of the light stood watch against the darkness, and cared for those who have been crippled by the attacks of sin's beasts.

# From Upside Down to Rightside Up

That is why Jesus' little team of disciples is the vanguard of heaven's restorative civilization. And the leading quality which identifies them is love. Here is where civilization begins in the dark jungles of earth.

### The Accent Of Heaven

A scene from Tony Campolo's life makes us think about this in fresh ways. When Tony spoke at a conference in Hawaii, it took a while for his body to catch up with the move across five time zones. The first night, his internal clock buzzed at three in the morning, and his stomach growled for attention.

Tony wandered quiet Honolulu streets looking for a place to get fried eggs and bacon. All the respectable places were closed and Tony finally ended up at a greasy dive in a narrow and dim alley. The place reeked with grunge. Tony was afraid to touch the menu for fear that it would stick to his fingers and that if he opened it something with too many legs to count might crawl out.

The guy behind the counter growled at him. "What d'ya want?"

Suddenly Tony wasn't hungry, no matter how much his stomach protested. He saw a stack of donuts under a cracked plastic cover. "I'll have a donut and a coffee," he said. That ought to be safe.

The guy poured a cup of dark, thick coffee. Then he wiped his greasy hand on his dirty apron, grabbed a donut with his fingers and threw it on the counter in front of Tony. There sat Tony Campolo, gagging on sour coffee and a stale donut.

All at once the door slammed open and eight or nine prostitutes sauntered in, just finished with a night's work. The joint was small and when the women crowded at the counter, they surrounded Tony, swearing, smoking and gossiping tales of their Johns. Another gulp and bite, and Tony would scram.

But something stopped his exit when the woman next to him turned to her friend and said, with a faraway look in her eye, "You know what? Tomorrow's my birthday. I'm gonna be thirty-nine..."

104

The other woman got nasty. "So what d'ya want from me?" she said. "A birthday party? Ya want me to get you a cake that says 'Happy Birthday' on it?"

The first woman whimpered a bit and replied, "Awe, come on! Why do ya have to be so mean? I was just tellin' you, that's all. You do ya have to put me down? I don't want anything from you! I mean, why should you give me a birthday party? I've never had a birthday party in my whole life! Why should I have one now?"

That got Tony thinking. He stayed until the women left, then said to the fellow behind the counter, "Do they come in here every night?"

"Yep," said the man. "Every night."

Tony asked him if he knew the one who had sat next to him. "Sure, that's Agnes. She's been coming here for years."

"Well," said Tony, "she just said that it was her birthday tomorrow. What do you think? You think you and I could do something about that — maybe throw her a birthday party right here tomorrow night?"

The man got a cute smile on his chubby cheeks. "That's great!" he said. So they made their plans. Tony would be back at 2:30 the next morning. He said he would help decorate the place and bring a birthday cake. "No way!" retorted the man. "My name's Harry and this is my place, and around here I make the cakes!"

At 2:30 the next morning Tony was back. He brought crepe paper decorations and a fold-out sign that said **Happy Birthday Agnes!** By 3 o'clock, the diner was looking pretty good. By 3:15 it was crowded with wall-to-wall prostitutes. Harry's wife had gotten the word out on the streets and every Honolulu streetwalker showed up.

At 3:30 Agnes and her group walked in. Tony had everyone ready for a shout, "Happy birthday, Agnes!" She was flabbergasted. Her mouth fell open, her legs wobbled, she put her hands to her head and almost fell over stunned. Her friend grabbed her by the arm and led her to the counter where her birthday cake rested on a pedestal. Tony led the room in an energetic chorus of "Happy Birthday To You."

# From Upside Down to Rightside Up

Agnes began to cry. She saw the cake with all the candles and wept. Harry, who was not used to seeing a prostitute cry, said rather gruffly, "Blow out the candles, Agnes! Come on! Blow out the candles! If you don't blow 'em out, I'll have to do it!"

So Agnes composed herself, and after a minute or two she blew them out. Everyone cheered. "Cut the cake, Agnes," they yelled. "Cut the cake!"

But Agnes looked down at the cake and, without taking her eyes off it, said to Harry, "Look, Harry... Would it be all right with you if I... I mean, is it okay if I... What I mean is, do you think it's be okay if I just *kept* the cake for a little while? I mean, is it all right if we don't eat it right away?"

Harry didn't know what to say. He shrugged his shoulders and said, "Sure, if that's what you want. Go ahead and keep the cake. Take it home if you want to."

Agnes turned to Tony and asked again, "Is it okay? I live just down the street. Can I take the cake home for a minute? I'll be right back. Honest!"

Agnes picked up the cake like it was the holy grail itself. Slowly she promenaded through the room with it high in front of her for everyone to see. She carried her treasure out the door and everyone there watched her in stunned silence. When she was gone nobody seemed to know what to do, so Tony got up on a chair and said, "What do you say we pray?"

There they were together in a hole-in-the-wall greasy spoon, all the prostitutes of Honolulu's streets, at 3:30 in the morning, and Tony gathered them to pray for Agnes. He prayed for her life. He prayed for her health. He prayed for her soul and her relationship with God.

When Tony finished praying Harry leaned over the counter and said, accusingly, "Hey! You never told me you was a preacher! What kind of a church do you belong to anyway?"

Tony replied, "I belong to a church that throws parties for prostitutes at 3:30 in the morning."

Harry thought about that for a moment and then said, "Naw you don't! There ain't no church like that! If there was, I'd join it!

Yessir, I'd be a member of a church like that!"

What do you think? Would you be a member of a church like that? Is this a church like that?

## Circles Of Life

A friend's son was very shy, Dale Galloway wrote in *Dream a New Dream*. Chad was usually by himself, and others took no effort to include him in their circles of friends. Every afternoon Chad's mother would see the children would pile off the school bus in groups, laughing, playing, and joking around with each other. Chad, however, always be the last down the steps, always alone. No one ever paid much attention to him.

One day in late January, Chad came home and said, "You know what, Mom? Valentine's Day is coming and I want to make a valentine for everyone in my class!"

Chad's mother told Dale how terrible she felt. "Oh no!" she thought. "Chad is setting himself up for a fall now. He's going to make valentines for everyone else but nobody will think of him. He'll come home all disappointed and just pull back further into his shell."

But Chad insisted, so they got paper and crayons and glue. Chad made 31 valentine cards. It took him three weeks.

The day he took them to school, his mother cried a lot. When he came off the bus alone as usual, bearing no valentine cards from others in his hands, she was ready for the worst.

Amazingly Chad's face was glowing. He marched through the door triumphant. "I didn't forget anybody!" he said. "I gave them all one of my hearts!"

That day Chad gained something more than just friends. He gained a sense of himself. He won a sense of dignity and worth. "I gave them all one of my hearts!" he said.

That is the accent of heaven in our earthly speech. That is the first sign of re-creation civilization. Edwin Markham, Oregon's onetime poet laureate pictured it powerfully:

> *He drew a circle that shut me out —*
> *Heretic! Rebel! A thing to flout!*

# From Upside Down to Rightside Up

> *But Love and I had the wit to win:*
> *We drew a circle that took him in.*
>                              (in the public domain)

Circles of hatred are erased by circles of love. Circles of judgment are blurred by widening circles of mercy. Circles of death give way to circles of life. The Bible says that when we had drawn God out of our circles, divine love drew us in. Perhaps Edwin Markham's poem could be translated into the conversation of heaven as the Father and the son reflect about us:

> *He drew a circle that shut us out —*
> *Heretic! Rebel! A thing to flout!*
> *But our love alone had the wit to win:*
> *We drew a circle that took him in!*
>                              (in the public domain)

That is the beginning of true civilization. When you listen to people like that, you know they are Jesus' disciples, and speak with the accent of heaven.

What do others see when you act, and hear when you speak?

# Glowing Network

During World War II, many members of the Lutheran church in Germany lost their faith because Hitler seduced them into ways of living that kept them from practicing their faith. But there was one man whom Hitler could not compromise. His name was Martin Niemöller. During World War I, Niemöller had been a great hero in the German military but when the Second World War came, he refused to bow to the authorities. He was marching to a different drumbeat. And march he did. When Hitler could not make him change his tune, could not bring him in line with the Nazis' brutal policies, Hitler had Niemöller thrown into a concentration camp.

Seven years later, when Niemöller came out of the camp, this is what he said: "Christianity is not an ethic, nor is it a system of dogmatics, but a living thing." Everyone who saw the fruits of his life knew who he was and where he stood and how he built his reputation.

Niemöller was a disciple of Jesus. Like those who share the final meal with their Lord, in the setting of our "Farewell Discourse" text, Niemöller experienced the "troubling" of the world that Jesus foretold. But he also knew the empowering of the Paraclete, the Holy Spirit of God, who bring remembrance and courage and hope.

## Waging Grace

Sometimes it seems fashionable to downplay our faith, to show ourselves in tune with our world, to treat Christianity flippantly. "Don't become a fanatic," we say. "Don't go overboard with religion. I believe in my heart; just don't ask me to make a big deal of it."

# From Upside Down to Rightside Up

But our faith is a big deal — or its no deal at all. Our relationship with God is everything or nothing. According to Jesus, we either develop the habit of deep faith or we get stuck in the habits of the world. This is what Jesus' disciples needed to know on the eve of his departure.

Jesus prophesied that they and we would have these times of loneliness in the world. That does not mean that either Jesus or the Father is unknowing or uncaring. It simply means that life is tough. What keeps us going in the right direction has got to be the call of eternity that assures us of a resolution which transcends all of the garbage we have to deal with now. This is the teaching of the Paraclete. It is the presence of peace that grows in the soil of adversity.

Some years ago, Fred Ferre spoke to a group of theology students about the source of his father's faith. His father was Nels Ferre, a distinguished theologian and author.

Nels came from a family of ten in Sweden. At thirteen, he was sent to find his future in America on his own. At the train station on the day of his departure, Nels' family surrounded him, holding hands as his father led in prayer. Then each member of the family said a prayer. That was his last earthly contact with his family.

Nels boarded the train and sat by the window, watching his family wave to him and cry. As the train rolled out of the station, his mother ran down the wooded platform alongside it. He slid the window open and leaned out just in time to hear her calling, "Nels! Nels! Remember Jesus! Remember Jesus!"

## Remember Jesus

That is what we are doing in these brief moments together, during the season of Easter: we are remembering Jesus. We are remembering God's love for us. We are remembering what it means to be what we were meant to be.

When the Danish novelist George Brandes was a young man, he looked up to Henrik Ibsen. Ibsen was much older that Brandes, but he took noticed of the young writer. Once Brandes asked the famous dramatist for help and encouragement.

Ibsen wrote a long letter in response, sharing this advice: If you want to serve your world, you have to look inside first. You have to find out what you're made of. You have to mine the depths of your own heart.

Then you have to be true to yourself, letting your faith shine for others. Said Ibsen, "There is no way in which you can benefit society more than by coining the metal you have in yourself."

He was right. No Christian can bring anything of true value to his world by putting on airs, by denying the grace of God within, or by keeping the power of the Spirit locked up. Pious hypocrisy is of no benefit to the world.

We're always eager to talk about the worst in society — corruption, greed, shams, materialism. Are we also eager to talk about the best of God within us? The strength of those who hold weak hands and trembling knees? The generosity of those who break bread with the poor? The courage of those who say "No" when the rage of the world says "Yes" or of those who, by faith in God say "Yes" when the scoffers of the world say "No"?

Think of Horatio Spafford, a lawyer in Chicago in the latter half of the nineteenth century. When Mrs. O'Leary's cow overturned the lantern the night of October 8, 1871, the great fire that resulted destroyed Spafford's home and business. These disasters put a heavy strain on the family. Mrs. Spafford became so nervous and run-down that her doctor recommended a vacation, so the family laid plans to sail for Europe in November of 1873.

As the date approached, Horatio realized he was too busy to leave with his family. He sent his wife and four daughters on ahead, planning to catch up with them later.

On November 22, the ship carrying the five Spafford women sank beneath the waves of the north Atlantic. Nearly everyone on board died. On December 1, Mrs. Spafford sent a telegram to Horatio from Cardiff, Wales. It said, "Saved alone!"

How much more would one couple have to suffer? Where was God in all of this?

Horatio left immediately to join his wife. As he crossed the Atlantic, he asked the captain to show him where the other ship

# From Upside Down to Rightside Up

had gone down. When they came to the spot, Horatio stood at the rail, looking out at the cruel gray sea. Did he cry out to God in pain? Probably so. Did he feel cheated by life? Undoubtedly. Did he turn away from God, saying God had let him down?

He could have. But he did not, because in those moments he wrote these words:

*When peace like a river attendeth my way,*
*when sorrows like sea billows roll;*
*whatever my lot, thou has taught me to say,*
*"It is well, it is well with my soul."*
*Though Satan should buffet, though trials should come,*
*let this blest assurance control;*
*that Christ has regarded my helpless estate,*
*and has shed his own blood for my soul.*
*O Lord, haste the day when my faith shall be sight,*
*the clouds be rolled back as a scroll;*
*the trump shall resound and the Lord shall descend;*
*even so, it is well with my soul.*

(in the public domain)

So we carry on, as he did, living by faith in a troubling world, trusting in Jesus through the power of the Paraclete. Horatio and Anna Spafford actually moved to Jerusalem after those events. They spent the last decades of their lives establishing a community of reconciliation between Jews, Muslims, and Christians in the heart of that troubled city.

So how is Jesus living in us here? What do others know of the power of the Paraclete who shines through us into a troubled world?

There is a glowing network spreading from this place, isn't there? How is your connection?

Ascension of Our Lord

**Luke 24:44-53**

# The Captain's Voice

I was walking through a building on a college campus when I spied a student lounging in an overstuffed chair, feet propped against a wall, reading a book that I had written. "That's my book!" I said too loudly and suddenly, amazed to find someone eyeballing my words.

With a start, she glared at me as if I were crazy.

"This is mine!" she said. "I just bought it at the bookstore."

I apologized, and then explained to her that I was the author of the volume she held. She was amazed and my ego was stroked, and she even wanted me to autograph her copy. Then, she wanted to know why I had written it.

### The Story Of The Bible

There is always a story behind the story, isn't there? Every book is crafted in passion, hammered out in hope, or scripted in the fevers of a message that has to be communicated.

Except for the Bible, of course. Often the Bible seems to be above all that because it is God's book. It is a holy book, a volume that existed from before beginnings, without a publisher's contract or seventeen editorial drafts or a book-signing promotional tour. Yet within the Bible's own pages, there are hints about its own story of beginnings.

Of course, we should turn to Genesis to find the Bible's beginnings, shouldn't we? After all, "Genesis" itself means "beginnings" or "origins." Yet if we read through Genesis, it is striking that nothing is said about the Bible. For instance, important as he was to biblical history, Adam had no "Bible." Nor did Noah, during all those years that he tried to hear a voice speaking of impending world destruction. Even Abraham, whose story is so central to the biblical record in both testaments, was not guided by a collection of sacred writings to which he could turn for devotional reflection each morning.

In clear and unambiguous testimony, the Bible's own internal evidence proves that the writing down of important ideas and history as a source book of revelatory insight had begun when the Israelites encountered God in a unique way at Mt. Sinai. It was there, according to the pages of Exodus, that God and Moses collaborated to create written documents which would travel with the community that became the nation of Israel.

It is imperative to understand more clearly what was taking place at Mount Sinai. In that moment of human history, God formally claimed Israel as partner in whatever the divine mission was for planet Earth. Israel, in turn, owned God as divine king and sovereign. In effect, God and Israel were married, and their starter home (the tabernacle) was built at the center of the Israelite camp.

## Covenant

Perhaps surprisingly, then, it appears that the Bible got its start as a political document. One of dominant civilizations of the ancient world was the Hittite kingdom. Somewhat secluded in the mountainous plateaus of Anatolia (eastern Turkey today), the Hittites shaped a vast web of international relations which at the height of their power in the fourteenth century BC, encompassed most of the ancient near east. The Hittites lingered in archaeological and historical studies for, among other things, their written code, used in defining international relations.

What makes this bit of ancient historical trivia so intriguing for Bible scholars is the uncanny correspondence between the elements of this Hittite covenant code and the literature at the heart of Israel's encounter with God at Sinai. The striking resonance between the usual form of the Hittite Suzerain-Vassal Covenant and the first speech of Yahweh to Israel at Mount Sinai binds the beginnings of conscious Israelite religion in terms other than that of a Suzerain (Yahweh) — Vassal (Israel) covenant making ceremony. In fact, this helps us think about the way in which the first biblical documents came into being and were used. They were initially written as covenant documents formulating the relationship between a nation and the (divine) ruler who earned the right in battle, to order their world.

This is why the word "covenant" becomes an essential term for all the rest of the literature that will be gathered into the collection eventually known as the Bible. The Bible begins with a covenant-making ceremony that produces certain documents, and then continues to grow as further expressions and implications of that covenant relationship are generated.

One can read theology, ethics, politics, or history out of the Bible, but one cannot do so while ignoring the essential role of the Sinai covenant between Yahweh and Israel. Even the idea of "kingdom," so prevalent and pervasive in the Bible, is built on the covenant idea, for it is by way of the covenant that Israel becomes the dominion of the great king. The kingdom of God is the context for all that is portrayed in the Bible, but the covenant is the administrative document through which the kingdom takes hold in the human societies which form the front ranks of Yahweh's citizenry.

### Where Are We Headed?

This is why Jesus talks to the two on the road the way he does. "He opened their minds so they could understand the Scriptures…" What are the scriptures? Jesus goes on to explain the central message of the law and the prophets and the Psalms. First came God's engagement with Israel at Mount Sinai. Then, for many centuries God spoke through the prophets, and their words became the Old Testament. God's people responded with psalms, hymns, and spiritual songs, worshiping the one at the center of all things.

And yet, Jesus said, it was all about him. We need to know why God did what God did and said what God said. But we also need to know that in more recent times, God stepped into our world in the person of Jesus Christ.

That is why our Bibles have two parts to them. There is an "Old" Testament that tells us about God's special relationship with ancient Israel; the significance of their marriage and mission. Then, added to it, is the "New" Testament, in which the story of Jesus is told and explained.

That is the story behind the story for the Bible. While we cannot run down to the bookstore for an autograph signing, it is likely that if we pay close attention as we read, we can carry on a pretty good conversation with the author.

### The Captain's Voice

Someone has suggested a powerfully illuminating analogy. When a ship is built, each part has a little voice of its own. As seamen walk the passageways on her maiden voyage, they can hear the creaking whispers of separate identities: "I'm a rivet!" "I'm a sheet of steel!" "I'm a propeller!" "I'm a beam!" For a while, these little voices sing their individual songs, proudly independent and fiercely self-protective.

But then a storm blows in on the high seas and the waves toss, the gales hurl, and the rain beats. If the parts of the ship try to withstand the pummeling independent from one another, each would be lost. On the bridge, however, stands the captain. He issues orders that take all of the little voices and bring them together for a larger purpose. By the time the vessel has weathered the storm, sailors hear a new and deeper song echoing from stem to stern: "I am a ship!"

It is the captain's call that creates the deeper identity. So too in our lives, according to Jesus. We can hear many voices in the Bible. Moses is there, and so are Isaiah and David. The law and the prophets guide our lives and keep us sailing. But ultimately the voice that matters is that of the captain. That is why Jesus said that all of scripture explained him, and he explained all of scripture.

A very creative friend once explained it like this: in a dream, he saw a marvelous apparatus of yellow silk billowing in the breezes next to a cliff. It was a transportation device of some kind, though he could not see either engines or supports. Like a magical tent, it floated in space.

Inside was a man whose face seemed so familiar and

friendly that my friend knew immediately this was an intimate acquaintance. However, he could not seem to remember how they were associated, nor the man's name. The man, with a smile of warmth, invited him to step off the cliff into the contrivance and be carried on a delightful journey in the yellow tent.

But my friend was so intrigued by the device itself that he wanted to try it on his own. *He* wanted to pilot the magical airship. So when he entered the craft, he fought the man for control and pushed him out onto the cliff. Unfortunately, just as my friend felt the power of flight swell in his commanding grasp, the entire yellow tent began to collapse in on itself, and plummet to disaster below. No matter what he did, my friend could not make the "machine" fly. He cried out for help, and suddenly the man he had pushed out reappeared at his side. In that exact moment, the airship began to billow and slow its freefall. Soon they were soaring together.

Without a further thought, my friend knew that the strangely familiar man was Jesus. He also knew why Jesus said to him, "Don't you know that the power to fly is not found in the 'machine' nor in your skills as a pilot, but in me?"

None of us begins to soar in life until we meet Jesus. As Jesus explained on the road to Emmaus, the whole Bible is all about him.

# The Divine Mission

A friend of mine taught ethics at a Christian college. Several years ago, there was a scare on campus because a student had been raped. Since my friend wanted his students to deal with actual ethical situations, he began the next class session with a question: "If a friend came to your room in tears, telling how her date had just raped her, what is the first thing you would do to help her?"

After a moment's reflective silence one student raised her hand and asked, tentatively, "Pray?"

The whole class tittered in nervous laughter, relieved to have a spot of comic relief to ease the tension. Even my friend found himself smiling and shaking his head slightly. "Of course," he said, "but *then* what would you do?" For the next hour he led the gathering in an ethical discussion of social care for someone who had been deeply hurt.

When my friend got home that evening, he reflected on the class session and then began to grow restless. Why, at a Christian college, he thought, should the suggestion of helping someone by beginning with prayer be greeted with laughter? And why should even he, an ordained minister of the gospel and a Christian ethics professor, initially wave off the suggestion of prayer as simply a polite formality to be dispensed with before the real business of helping began? Why should prayer seem so insignificant and powerless?

### Does Prayer Work?

Jesus' prayer is powerful, of course, isn't it? I have always loved John 17, and this great prayer Jesus voiced. Over the years it has come to be known as Jesus' "high priestly prayer," because

Jesus stands with us and for us before the Father, begging and pleading for our lives to resonate with divine love. Yet did Jesus' own prayer work? Do we, who know these things, actually find them changing our behaviors? Does prayer, even Jesus' prayer, work?

These are important questions, for despite our pious talk we often treat prayer with apologetic skepticism. When I was a seminary student, one of the elders at the church where I was working decided to make a career move. He invited the pastor and me to a demonstration of a product promotion speech he was developing as he began a sales and distribution job with a nationally famous pyramid-like company. During our evening together, he played a tape of a motivational speech he had heard at a recent company rally. The most gripping speaker was a former pastor who now was a top sales distributor for this famous firm.

"I used to be a pastor," the man said, "and all I had to give people was prayer. When I was a pastor, I had a man come to me weeping for the tragedy of his life. 'I'm a poor fellow, pastor,' the man cried, 'and it is ruining my marriage. I can't make enough to buy my wife the things she wants, and our children feel out of place at school with their shabby clothes. Sometimes I think I should divorce my wife, because then she would get more money from the government than she gets from me. What should I do, pastor?'

"I felt so bad," said the former pastor, now turned top salesman. "At that time all I could offer the man was prayer. If only I knew then what I know now. If he came to me today, I could help him so much more!"

The crowd roared with approval and applauded that former pastor as if he were God. I think of that man's motivational speech every time I sit at the bedside of a terminally ill cancer patient. I think of that speech when I wrestle in prayer with a couple nearing divorce. I think of his words when I pray with a friend of mine whose life has been mostly depression and drugs. Does prayer help? Is it more an exercise in placating my uneasy conscience than it is a true "first aid?" I wonder.

# From Upside Down to Rightside Up

### The Breath Of Heaven

Yet when I look back over my years of praying and being prayed over, I realize that there is also a larger picture to paint about prayer. For one thing, as Bishop William Temple said, "I don't know if prayer works, but I do know that when I stop praying, coincidences stop." I too have found that truth in my life. Although I cannot document every exact answer to prayer, I do know that unseen forces have often assisted me and those I have prayed with in ways beyond rational explanation. Even the medical community has recognized the healing power of prayer, as Dr. Lawrence Dossey has reported in several of his books.

Second, I think of the way that help comes best when we are children. I watched a young girl and boy collide while running through a hallway the other day, banging heads, and falling backward onto the floor. Each was stunned, momentarily, and then each looked around for a nearby parent. It was not until they spied caring mothers that each began a mighty and mournful wail. Not only that, but the crying from pain changed its tone when they each rested in the comfort of hugging arms—wails that earlier seemed edged with torment became whimperings seeking sympathy. A big part of prayer, it seems from scripture, has to do with finding our way into the care of a Father, even when the hurts and pains of life still trouble us.

Third, I think that Jesus is reminding his disciples, and us through them, that we are not alone in the universe, and that times of trouble are times of returning to our truest human condition of spiritual need. Jesus does not promise that all our fortunes will change because a magical prayer has been offered. Rather, he indicates that precisely when we are so troubled, the natural place for us to turn is outside of ourselves and to God. As M. Scott Peck put it in his powerful book, *A World Waiting to Be Born*, either we know the truth of our spiritual need or we spend our lives playing games with ourselves and others that steal the best of who we are away from us.

### Transforming Grace

I think of Fred. Fred was a big man with a big heart. His life had been ringed with tragedy, but he had grown through it and chose to spend his last career years as a missionary in Africa. A few years later he was returned to our town near death. A brain tumor had suddenly appeared and quickly robbed him of speech and motor control. He was hospitalized for several weeks and then released to die at home.

We prayed much for Fred. We shared the personal and family needs through a wide web of Christian contacts. We held specific healing services and added Fred's condition to our weekly prayer bulletin.

Despite our best desires, we gradually became aware that only death would bring divine healing. Fred's life this side of eternity was too far destroyed for recovery.

I made regular visits to the small house that Fred's wife purchased. Mostly Fred lay in bed moaning and restless. While his muscles contorted horribly, his skin began to turn unhuman shades of gray. Several times the family members, scattered at some distance, were called together for what appeared to be "the end."

On one of these occasions, I stood with them in a circle around Fred's bed. Fred was greatly agitated and moaned incomprehensibly. I read a Psalm and a promise from Paul, and then we prayed together, holding hands, asking God to take Fred home soon. It only seemed, however, that Fred's inner restlessness got worse. I stepped closer to the bed and placed my hand on his forehead. I spoke directly to him the blessing he himself had pronounced over God's people so many times: "The Lord bless you and keep you, Fred. The Lord make his face shine upon you. The Lord smile upon you and give you his peace" (Numbers 6:24-26).

Immediately Fred settled peacefully, his muscles relaxing and his labored breath easing. "You can go home now, Fred," I said. Each family member held Fred's hands briefly, speaking words of care release. I walked out of the house. Before I could drive away, Fred slipped into eternity.

Keep Fred's story in mind as I take you on another pastoral

visit, happening at the same time. LaVern struggled with open sores on her legs, among several different ailments. She was in great pain most always and alternated between weeks of sitting in a lounge chair with her legs elevated and periods of aggressive treatment in the hospital. We prayed together regularly over the telephone, and now and then I would sit with her for an hour, sharing the whimsy of life. Few people I knew have endured as much pain and heartbreak as has LaVern. Yet fewer still have developed as joyful an outlook on the many small graces of existence.

One day LaVern called me with a new request. She wanted me to come over with an elder of the church to anoint her with oil. I called one of the elders, a trusted prayer partner, and we gathered around LaVern's chair. First, we spent time confessing to one another, then we spent time in prayer. We shared the bread and cup of the sacrament, seeking intimacy with Jesus and one another in the body. We touched the sores on LaVern's legs and begged for healing. Then I took the oil and rubbed it gently over LaVern's wounds, commanding them, in the name of Jesus, to be healed. We gave God thanks for the healing he was bringing and would accomplish, and I spoke the same blessing I had pronounced over Fred.

There was no "electric shock" moving through my fingers or LaVern's legs, nor any immediate end to the weeping from the skin openings. Yet in the next week, a remarkable change took place, both in the peace that infused LaVern's heart and the clear closures of the wounds. Her doctors put off scheduled surgery and several months later LaVern came to Sunday worship for the first time in a year, standing on her own legs.

LaVern's struggles with those sores continued over the years, and she called for intercession many times. Now and again we looked back to the day we met together with the elders of the church and anointed her wounds as a watershed moment. LaVern believed she experienced a special healing in that moment. I think so too.

I also think Fred was healed in the moment of our touch at his bedside, though in a different way. There is power for life in the gospel of Jesus that sometimes works through the medical industries of our culture and sometimes works despite them. There is nothing in the Bible to call into question a Christian's use of doctors and prescription medications. But neither does the Bible tell us that doctors are the true great physician. Whenever healing happens, God has smiled. And that is why intercession matters.

### Spreading Love

Sometimes in small moments of care, sometimes in consequential movements of socially transforming "great awakenings," the prayer of Jesus in John 17 unfolds in our lives. When Geoffrey Wainwright wrote a summary of his theology, he called the resulting work *Doxology*, a song of praise to God. But he found all his words inadequate to convey what his theology meant for living. So he pulled his doctrinal treatises together with this concluding story:

Many years ago, Turkish soldiers raided an Armenian home. The officer in charge ordered the parents killed and gave the daughters to his soldiers to be raped and brought home as slaves. He kept the oldest daughter for himself, using her again and again in despicable ways.

One day, the oldest daughter escaped. After she found her life again, she trained to be a nurse. But when she was finally assigned to a hospital, she discovered that her ward was filled with Turkish officers.

Late one night, her old enemy was brought in. By the light of the lantern, she could see he was near death. She would not have to try to kill him — with a little neglect, he would be gone.

But the man did not die. As the days passed, he recovered strength. One morning the doctor told him how fortunate he was. The doctor pointed to the young nurse and said, "But for her devotion to you, you would be dead."

Recognizing her, the officer asked, "Why didn't you kill me?" She simply replied, "I am a follower of him who said, `Love your enemies.'"

Yes indeed. .

www.ingramcontent.com/pod-product-compliance
Lightning Source LLC
Chambersburg PA
CBHW031859090426
42741CB00005B/562